FRÉMONT

Soldier, Explorer, Statesman

J.C. Fremont.

FRÉMONT

Soldier, Explorer, Statesman

By

FREDRIKA SHUMWAY SMITH

ILLUSTRATED WITH PHOTOGRAPHS & MAPS

✠

Rand McNally & Company

CHICAGO • NEW YORK • SAN FRANCISCO

THIS BOOK has been written to honor all explorers who, like John Charles Frémont, fearlessly ventured into unknown lands, crossing dangerous river torrents, climbing towering heights of impassable mountains, subduing tribes of hostile savages. All these courageous men risked their lives to open a way across our continent, so that following generations could travel safely. Frémont, the "Pathfinder," typifies their achievements, and his story is a fascinating chapter in the annals of the West.

Contents

CO. SCHOOL

✠ C697291

1. BORN TO ADVENTURE 9
2. UP THE MISSISSIPPI AND THE MISSOURI . . 21
3. JESSIE 43
4. THROUGH THE SOUTH PASS
   TO FRÉMONT'S PEAK 49
5. JESSIE DEFIES THE ARMY 68
6. TO OREGON 75
7. ACROSS THE SIERRAS IN WINTER 86
8. HERO'S HOMECOMING 106
9. THE ROAD TO WAR 118
10. THE FIGHT WITH THE KLAMATHS 133
11. THE BEAR FLAG WAR AND
    THE CONQUEST OF CALIFORNIA 144
12. CONFLICT WITH KEARNY AND
    COURT MARTIAL 155
13. DEATH IN THE SNOW 167
14. GOLD FOR THE SENATOR FROM CALIFORNIA . 178
15. FIRE, AND RETREAT TO EUROPE 187

16. THE FIFTH, AND LAST, EXPEDITION 195

17. FRÉMONT FOR PRESIDENT 201

18. A LITTLE WAR, AND
    THE BEGINNING OF A GREAT ONE . . . 212

19. UNHAPPY COMMANDER 217

20. DISASTER 236

21. THE END OF A LONG TRAIL 244

    Index 251

Photographs & Maps

✠

John C. Frémont FRONTIS

Joel Poinsett 16

Buffalo hunt 37

Lost on the prairie 39

Thomas Hart Benton 45

Fort Laramie 57

Flag on Frémont Peak 62

Passage down the Platte 65

Kit Carson 78

Captain Sutter 97

Sutter's Fort 99

President Polk 112

Delaware bodyguard 115

Bent's Fort 120

"In the blaze of the fire, was an old woman" 122

Sagundai 125

Night assault 136

Lake Klamath 141

The Bear Guidon and the Bear Flag 147

Brigadier General Kearny 160

A terrific snowstorm 172

President Zachary Taylor 183

Jessie Benton Frémont 189

Frémont riding through fire 197

Newspaper cartoons 206

Francis Preston Blair and Montgomery Blair 227

MAPS

Missouri and Mississippi rivers, and Louisiana Purchase 24

Frémont Expeditions, 1837 and 1839 33

The Spanish, Santa Fe and, Oregon Trails, and Frémont Expeditions, 1842–1846 116

Frémont Expeditions, 1848–1849 198

ACKNOWLEDGMENTS

The sources of the photographs in this book are: Frontispiece and page 62, from *Memoir of the Life and Public Services of John Charles Frémont* by John Bigelow; pages 16 and 120, U.S. Signal Corps photos in National Archives; pages 65, 172, and 197, from *Kit Carson's Life and Adventures* by Dewitt C. Peters; pages 112, 160, 183, and 227, U.S. Signal Corps photos (Brady Collection) in National Archives; pages 115 and 136 from *Life, Explorations, and Public Services of John Charles Frémont* by Charles Wentworth Upham; page 147, from *Frémont, the World's Greatest Adventurer* by Allan Nevins; page 189 from *Souvenirs of My Time* by Jessie Benton Frémont; page 206, Courtesy of The New York Historical Society, New York City. All others are from *Memoirs of My Life* by John Charles Frémont.

The maps were drawn especially for this book by Fred Kliem; the jacket illustration is by Lorence F. Bjorklund.

Born to Adventure

✠

RAVEL, ADVENTURE, AND a natural curiosity about places and people were in his blood. His father, also John Charles Frémont, when a young man, had fled from a village near Lyons, France, during the reign of terror that had accompanied the French Revolution. He had sailed on a French ship for Santo Domingo (now Trujillo), where he planned to live with an aunt. But the ship was captured by a British cruiser and taken to one of the British West Indies. Young John Charles was interned with the other passengers.

Apparently the internees were given a certain amount of freedom, for Frémont was allowed to eke out his scanty prison allowance by making baskets, upholstering furniture, and painting frescoes in the houses of some of the wealthy inhabitants of the city. In due time he got away—whether by release or escape is uncertain—and found his way to Norfolk, Virginia.

Penniless on arrival, but speaking fluent English, he turned his knowledge of two languages to account by giving private lessons in French. It was at a time when the freedom-loving revolutionary French people were held in high regard in America. It was a mark of fashion —what might now be called "a status symbol"—to be able to speak the language, so the young refugee lacked neither pupils nor friends in high circles. Later he went to Richmond and taught in the academy of Louis Girardin, a friend of Thomas Jefferson. It was while he was here that he met, and fell in love with, the woman who was later to become John Charles Frémont's mother.

The former Anne Beverly Whiting was the youngest daughter of Colonel Thomas Whiting, who was a leading member of the House of Burgesses of Virginia, and a relative of George Washington. She was considered one of the most beautiful young women in Virginia. Charles and Anne were young and impetuous. They eloped, on July 10, 1811, leaving Richmond behind them, driving their own horse and carriage. This was the start of a period of happy traveling throughout the South. Each night they stopped wherever they happened to be, sometimes sleeping in a tent, sometimes in an Indian village, sometimes at an inn. Frémont may have found work here and there as a fresco painter, upholsterer, and teacher of French.

It was while the happy young couple were still living this somewhat gypsy-like existence that John Charles Frémont, their first child, was born in Savannah, Georgia, on January 21, 1813.

Charles and Anne later had a second son, and then a daughter. When John Charles was five years old his father died, and his mother settled in Charleston, South Carolina, a city of about 20,000 people—one of the most picturesque and fashionable of the old South. There were gay balls, Philharmonic concerts, graceful carriages drawn by high-stepping horses driven by uniformed coachmen. There were fashionably dressed ladies with their lacy parasols. There was race week, with its carnival spirit. There were the Negro slaves whose gay chatter and songs were heard on the streets and on the wharves, where barrels of molasses, bags of coffee, cocoanuts, and bananas from the West Indies were unloaded, and rice and cotton were loaded for export.

Young Frémont's mother was a poor widow, and his father had been an equally poor roving immigrant. But the social standing of Anne's family, the Whitings, was sufficient to insure courteous treatment and hospitality for the little family from the most aristocratic of their neighbors. And John Charles easily won friends with his keen and active mind, his quick and ready friendliness, and his eager interest in everything and everybody, which of course made others interested in him.

One of those who became interested was John W. Mitchell, a prominent lawyer of Charleston. Mitchell was so impressed by the handsome boy's mind, his quickness at learning, and his apparently instinctive good breeding, that he offered him a place in his law office, where the young Frémont for a time looked forward—perhaps without much enthusiasm—to becoming a member of the South Carolina bar. And then, in an excess of friendliness, the attorney decided that the boy's eager interest in literature would be wasted in a law office, that his eloquence would find a better setting in a pulpit than in a courtroom. Therefore, John Charles was sent, at the age of fourteen, to a preparatory school run by one Dr. John Robertson, who specialized in getting boys ready for entrance into Charleston College.

Some years later Dr. Robertson, in an introduction that he wrote to his translation of Xenophon's *Anabasis*, described John Charles Frémont at fourteen in the somewhat flowery language of the day:

. . . of middle size, graceful in manners, rather slender, but well formed, and upon the whole what I should call handsome; of a keen piercing eye, and a noble forehead, seemingly the very seat of genius. . . . Intelligence beamed in his dark eye, and shone brightly on his countenance, indicating great ability and an assurance of his future progress. I at once put him in the highest class, just beginning to read Caesar's *Commentaries,* and . . . his prodigious memory and enthusiastic application soon enabled him to pass the best. He began Greek at the same time . . . . In the space of one year he had with the class and at odd hours he had with myself, read four books of Caesar, Cornelius Nepos, Sallust, six books of Virgil, nearly all Horace, and two books of Livy; and in Greek, all of *Graeca Minora,* about the half of the first volume of *Graeca Majora,* and four books of Homer's *Iliad.*

One cannot help wondering whether the lad had time for anything except Greek and Latin!

Dr. Robertson continued:

I have hinted that he was designed for the church, but

when I contemplated his bold, fearless disposition, his powerful inventive genius, his admiration of warlike exploits, and his love of heroic and adventurous deeds, I did not think it likely that he would be a minister of the Gospel. . . . When the Greek class read the account that Herodotus gives of the battle of Marathon, the bravery of Miltiades and his ten thousand Greeks raised his patriotic feelings to enthusiasm and drew from him expressions which I thought were embodied a few days afterward in some well-written verses in a Charleston paper . . . and suspecting my talented scholar to be the author, I . . . asked him if he did not write them, and hesitating at first rather blushingly, he confessed he did.

Dr. Robertson also recorded the rapid progress young Frémont made in mathematics, and the remarkable fact that, after a year spent in this school, he was able to enter the Junior class in Charleston College.

Frémont's own memories of his school days were happy ones. To Dr. Robertson he wrote movingly many years later, "There is no time to which I go back with more pleasure than that spent with you." And he wrote in his *Memoirs* of two books that he read during his school years with the most absorbed interest, and commented on how greatly both had influenced his life. One was a chronicle of men who had made themselves famous by "brave and noble" deeds; the other was a work on practical astronomy, containing "beautifully clear maps of the stars, and many examples of astronomical calculations." In the many hours that he spent poring over the pages of the latter work, he made himself familiar with the night skies and the ordinary observations necessary to determine longitude and latitude. Without realizing it he was intensively gaining a knowledge and a skill that would be essential to him in the activities that dominated the greatest part of his adult life.

"Charley" Frémont was a good student—up to a point. While his main interest was in his books, he made rapid progress, driven by his restless curiosity about all things. He especially loved Greek which, he himself wrote later, "had a mysterious charm, as if behind the strange characters belonging to an ancient world I was to find things of wonderful interest." But he was not to be limited by Greek, Latin, mathematics, and the stars, for there were so many "things of wonderful interest" in young Charley's life.

One of them was Cecilia, whose Creole parents had escaped to Charleston from the Santo Domingo massacres which accompanied an uprising under Toussaint l'Ouverture. Cecilia, their oldest daughter, was a handsome girl, with jet black hair, clear skin, and large dark eyes. Young Frémont spent many hours with her and her two brothers—hours that his instructors thought might better have been spent on his books. The young people roved the woods outside the town, which were still much as they had been before any white man saw them, or sailed on the bay, sometimes through hazardous breakers that gave Frémont the peculiarly savage joy that physical danger was to bring him all of his life. Years later,

after an especially happy married life, he still remembered Cecilia with tenderness and wrote of her in his
Memoirs: "I lived in the glow of a passion that now I
know extended its refining influence over my whole life."

The authorities at the college were unsympathetic,
however. Frémont was given a stern warning, to which
he blithely paid no attention. Finally, only a few months
before graduation, he was dismissed for "habitual irregu-
larity and incorrigible negligence." This was on February 5, 1831.

His expulsion seemed to bother him no more than
the warning had. He continued his idling and his companionship with Cecilia and her brothers until, apparently, the relationship simply petered out, and he saw
that it was time for him to go to work.

For a while he taught mathematics in two private
schools, and then his desire to travel was gratified
through the happy influence of another patron, Joel R.
Poinsett, a botanist whose name is best known now for
the flower he developed—the red Poinsettia. Poinsett was
one of Charleston's most distinguished citizens. He had
been a member of Congress from 1821–25, Minister to
Mexico from 1825–29, and was later to become Secretary of War. At the time that Frémont met him, in 1833,
he was famous in Charleston for his "breakfasts." Here
once a week he entertained as his guests charming
women and men of importance in intellect and achieve-
ment. Young Frémont's eagerness, his personal charm,
and his obvious intelligence, attracted the older man,
and the twenty-year-old youth became one of the break-

Joel Poinsett

fast guests. At these breakfasts, John Charles poured into sympathetic ears his love of adventure and his eagerness to see the world.

As if in answer to his desire, the sloop-of-war *Natchez*, which for some months had been lying in the port of Charleston, was ordered to return to Hampton Roads, and from there to sail on a cruise to South America. When it left, young Frémont was aboard as a teacher of mathematics. His post had been obtained for him by his friend Joel Poinsett. Aboard, too, as executive officer of the ship, was Lieutenant David Farragut, who had been a midshipman on the *Essex* during the War of 1812.

The ship's company was saddened at Rio de Janeiro by the death of a midshipman in a foolish duel with one of his shipmates. When another duel was arranged between two other members of the ship's company, Mr. Lovell of South Carolina and Mr. Parrott of Massachusetts, Frémont was asked to act as second for Parrott, and Decatur Hurst, a friend of Frémont, was asked to second Lovell, a nephew of Poinsett. Hurst and Frémont then put their heads together and made a plan that, if it was successful, would avert a second tragedy.

On the appointed morning, the four men quietly left the ship in a small boat and rowed to a narrow strip of sandy beach, with Hurst and Frémont carrying the pistols, which they had loaded aboard ship. On shore, the two combatants, pistols in hand, took their positions twelve paces apart and, at the signal, fired point blank. The agreed-upon distance between them was so short that, when neither was even slightly wounded, their surprise seemed even greater than their undoubted relief. Immediately, Hurst and Frémont went to them, took their pistols, declared that the demands of honor had been satisfied and the affair was over. In silence they rowed back to the *Natchez,* going aboard as quietly as they had left. Only these four men knew that there had been a duel in the gray morning light. And only Hurst and Frémont knew that the two duelists had fired pistols loaded with powder only. For the two seconds, both intelligent and kindly young men, knowing how trivial the quarrel was, had arranged between them to so load for the first shot, and use all of their persuasion,

17

if it was necessary, to keep a second shot from being fired. If, however, the combatants insisted on it, they would reload on the site of the duel and add ball to the powder. Their humanity and common sense had won the day.

Back at Norfolk, Frémont applied for a newly created Navy post—Professor of Mathematics—and passed his examination. But meanwhile, perhaps through the influence of his friend Poinsett, he received the offer of another appointment, which pleased him better. Without a second thought, he declined the naval appointment that was offered him, and took the first steps toward the career that dominated most of his life.

A survey was to be made of a proposed route for a railroad between Charleston and Cincinnati. In charge was Captain W. S. Williams of the United States Topographical Corps. Under Captain Williams was a West Point graduate named White, and one of White's assistants was John Charles Frémont.

The job was scarcely finished, when a new opportunity offered itself.

But meanwhile another event took place. Was it Poinsett's gentle but influential hand that brought it about, or did the heads of Charleston College simply have sober second thoughts and decide to show appreciation, while he was on his way up, for a man destined to become famous? On March 19, 1836, a little over five years after the authorities had expelled him, the school conferred a Bachelor of Arts degree upon young Frémont. And so, when John Charles left Charleston for another adventure, he could put the letters B.A. after his name, if he chose to.

The government policy of moving all Indians living east of the Mississippi to new locations west of that mighty stream had been instituted by Thomas Jefferson, but had been carried out slowly during the succeeding administrations. The last to be moved were the Cherokees, who lived in a district where North Carolina, Tennessee, and Georgia came together in wild mountainous land, much of which had never been accurately mapped.

This tribe showed signs of resistance and, fearing an armed uprising, the Federal government asked Captain Williams, who had conducted the Charleston-Cincinnati project, to make a military survey of the region. This would serve a purpose in case of the unhappy necessities of war and facilitate a proper peacetime disposition of the lands in any case. Captain Williams, who had noticed Frémont's excellent work on the former expedition, invited him to come along as an assistant.

The survey was made during the winter of 1836–37. The men were divided into groups and each group was given a specific assignment. Frémont worked with two companions, Archie Campbell and Hull Adams. During their first night in the Indian Territory they walked into a situation that might have frightened timid men. Entering an Indian village, they found the men holding a feast, all drunk, riotously noisy, and full of fight. Frémont and his two companions probably paused, wondering how they could retreat without being noticed. But before they had time to do anything about it, friendly squaws, who had stayed sober, led them to a log cabin half filled with husked corn, and hid them there. All night they were kept awake by the cold, their uncomfortable beds, the rats that constantly ran over them, and the drunken shouts and cries of the noisy Indians. They welcomed the rising sun as a prisoner welcomes release, and gladly stole away from the village in which the carousers of the night before were now sleeping.

As the survey continued, they spent the nights in any accommodation they could find—sometimes in Indian cabins, sometimes in tents. Huge fires of hickory and oak logs were kept all night before their quarters, and their sleep was often punctuated by the cries of wildcats and the hooting of owls. Often they shot and ate wild pigs that roamed the area, fattening on chestnuts and acorns. Sometimes they were guests at Indian feasts at which their hosts would get drunk and slash each other wildly with knives, never flinching at the pain, nor paying attention to the blood that flowed as a result. But these occurrences were rare. In most of the villages and farms the inhabitants lived peacefully and welcomed Frémont and his companions with dignified hospitality.

The survey was an experience that Frémont was never to forget. Years later he wrote in his *Memoirs*: "Here I found the path which I was destined to walk. There were to be no more years wasted in tentative efforts to find a way for oneself. The work was laid out and it began here with a remarkable continuity of purpose."

Up the Mississippi
and the Missouri

✠

*A*FTER RETURNING from the Cherokee survey, Frémont had scarcely settled down to a visit with his mother, when, to his astonishment, he received notification from the Army that he had been given a commission as second lieutenant in the U. S. Topographical Corps. Accompanying the notice was an order directing him to report to the Secretary of War in Washington. He understood at once how his commission had come about, for the Secretary of War was his old friend Joel Poinsett. Plainly he had recommended his protegé to President Van Buren and asked for the appointment for some purpose of his own. Something was in the wind! Frémont's disappointment at having to leave his mother so quickly was tempered by his excitement and suspense over what Poinsett planned for him.

The map on page 24 shows the source of the Missouri River near Helena in Montana. From here it runs across Montana, through North Dakota and South Dakota, cutting off the northeast corner of what would undoubtedly have been a part of Nebraska if it had not been for the river, goes along the boundary line between Nebraska and Iowa, cornering Kansas and dividing it from Missouri, and across Missouri to its junction with the Mississippi, a little above St. Louis. The Mississippi, from this point, going northward, separates Missouri, Iowa, and a part of Minnesota from Illinois and Wisconsin. Somewhere northwest of Duluth the river is difficult to trace, but it is still there on the map, a thin line running northwest across Minnesota to a small lake called Itasca, the source of the mighty stream. With the Missouri it bounds a great area shaped roughly like an irregular triangle standing on its apex.

When Frémont was ordered to Washington, only Illinois and Missouri existed as states in this large expanse. Wisconsin was a territory, and Iowa was about to become one. The rest of the territory was simply a part of that tremendous tract of land called the "Province of Louisiana," which had been bought from France in 1803—a transaction that has been recorded in history as "the Louisiana Purchase." The extent of this vast realm is shown on the map on page 24; its price was $15 million! President Jefferson was strongly criticized for having "wasted" this tremendous sum on a wilderness!

The purchase consisted of approximately 1,038,000 square miles or 664,378,000 acres. Thus the United States paid a little more than two cents an acre for the lot!

It was not, however, merely as a bargain in real estate that President Jefferson had been interested in this vast expanse of land. England and Russia were both engaged in the fur trade, using Pacific Ocean ports from which to ship furs to the Orient. Jefferson envisaged an American port on the West Coast from which United States ships could sail to Asia, and an overland route to reach it.

But at the time practically nothing was known about the "Province of Louisiana." Not a single boundary had been clearly defined.

John B. McMaster wrote in *A History of the People of the United States:*

Meagre accounts of what travellers had seen on the Missouri, of what hunters and trappers knew of the upper Mississippi, of what the Indians said were the features of the great plains that stretched away toward the setting sun, had indeed reached officials, and out of these was constructed the most remarkable document any President has ever submitted to Congress. It told of a tribe of Indians of gigantic stature, . . . of land so fertile as to yield the necessities of life almost spontaneously, of an immense prairie covered with buffalo . . . and how, a thousand miles up the Missouri, was a vast mountain of salt!

This was hardly trustworthy information. Indeed, until 1837, no one knew the source of the Missouri.

A few years earlier than that a French mathematician and astronomer named Jean Nicholas Nicollet arrived in New Orleans. Impressed by the magnificent waterway that he saw flowing into the sea there, he became curious about where it came from and the nature of the country drained by its upper reaches and tributaries, partly be-

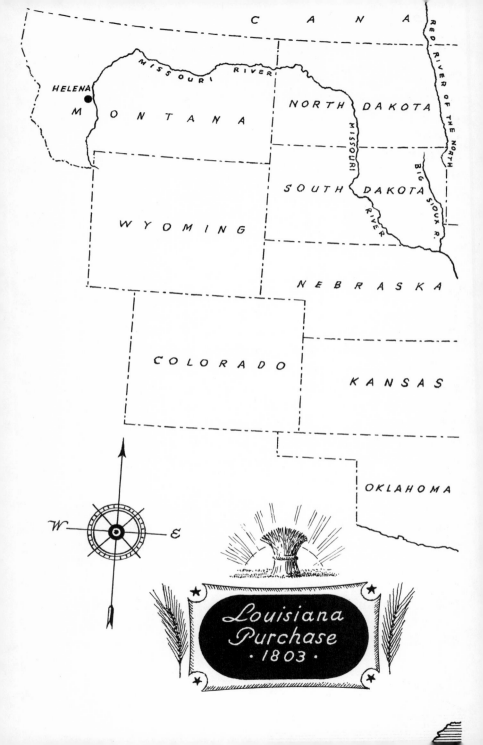

The Missouri and Mississippi rivers from source to mouth, and the Louisiana Purchase. State boundaries are shown as they are today. The Louisiana Purchase covered approximately the area now occupied by all of the states shown

cause it was his nature to be curious, and partly because, a French patriot, he wanted to reassert the French claims to credit for the explorations of LaSalle, Champlain, and others of his countrymen.

Others were also interested in the region, among them the War Department of the United States and the wealthy fur house of Chouteau and Company in St. Louis—the latter because the Indian country west of the Mississippi was rich in furs and thus a valuable source of supply. Chouteau and Company outfitted Nicollet and gave him financial support, the War Department lent him some scientific instruments and gave him letters to army officers and Indian agents on the frontier, and, in 1835, he was off.

The following year he returned, having reached the source of the Mississippi and traced the river, which at that point scarcely suggested the mighty stream it was to become farther to the south, some miles on its course. His work attracted the attention of Secretary of War Poinsett, the two men met, and a further expedition was arranged to explore and map the vast territory between the Mississippi and the Missouri, with Nicollet at its head, and the newly created Second Lieutenant John Charles Frémont as one of his assistants.

Frémont was delighted. Washington in the 1830's was not an inspiring place. Its one street of any importance—Pennsylvania Avenue—was either a sea of mud or a desert of dust, depending on the weather. The only friend Frémont had in the capital was Joel Poinsett, who was busy with the affairs of the War Department.

John Charles, whose strong body was used to vigorous exercise, felt frustrated and ill at ease in inactivity. Now he was to follow again the faint trails made by animals and Indians, fight his way through thick undergrowth where no trails existed, sleep in pine-scented forests beside fragrant campfires, hear the cries of the wild-cat and whippoorwill at night, be awakened by the singing of birds in the morning, and know the joy of living among the unspoiled beauties of nature. This, he knew now, was the life he wanted.

He knew, too, how much it could mean to him to be associated with the distinguished Nicollet, a polished French gentleman, and also a respected member of the French Academy of Sciences. From him, Frémont would be able to learn more about surveying and map-making, and his own mathematical ability would stand him in good stead here.

As soon as he had received his orders, he left Washington for St. Louis to join Nicollet. The first part of his trip was by stagecoach. Then he boarded a boat on the Ohio River that took him to the Mississippi, and there he changed to another, which carried him to St. Louis.

The population of St. Louis at this time was largely made up of Creole descendants of the original French colonists, backwoodsmen from Kentucky and Tennessee, traders from the Atlantic states, Indians and half-breeds from the prairies, boatmen of the Mississippi and Ohio rivers, and French-Canadian voyageurs. Frémont found his heart beating a little more strongly and his breath coming faster as he saw the Indians of various tribes loitering about the streets, or an occasional Kentucky hunter striding along with his rifle on his shoulder and knife in his belt. These were people from the kind of country he loved.

But there were also the old French mansions, finely built and indicating luxury and culture. Through their casement windows he could now and then hear the melody of a violin, the sound of billiard balls, or a happy voice singing an old French tune. St. Louis was a frontier town, but it was also a seat of culture on the edge of the great unknown, which stretched westward over many miles of unmapped territory. Here, while the house of Chouteau was equipping the Nicollet expedition, Frémont met and made friends with many distinguished persons already known to Nicollet. Among them was a young captain in the Engineering Corps named Robert E. Lee. The man who was destined to become Commander-in-Chief of the Confederate Army during the Civil War was supervising some improvements on the Mississippi River. Frémont was greatly impressed with the dignity and friendliness of his bearing and spoke highly of him in his *Memoirs*.

Finally equipped, and staffed with a group of voyageurs and a German botanist named Charles Geyer, whom Nicollet hired at his own expense, the expedition left to push its way up the Mississippi to the point at which it was not navigable to large boats—Fort Snelling, a military station and trading post of the American Fur Company, near the site of what is now St. Paul. Here they were the guests of Henry Sibley, a partner in

Astor's great fur business, who had charge of seven posts in the region, of which that at Fort Snelling was one.

He was a gracious host, a dog lover, and a hunter whose prowess was admired by the Indians, with whom he got on well. Within the enclosure about the house, Mr. Sibley had built a lookout platform about fifteen feet high with a parapet around the top of it, for a number of hunting dogs that he kept. Here the dogs would stand by the hour, ringing the parapet with their front paws and their heads.

Standing on the west bank of the Mississippi, Frémont could look across the river to the frame houses that marked a small settlement of whites in Wisconsin Territory. Near at hand on the west bank was a Sioux Indian village, and high on a bluff, between the Mississippi and the Minnesota rivers, stood Fort Snelling with the flag of the United States flying above its battlements. Frémont was standing at the dividing line between civilization and the unmapped wilderness. He wandered about the fort and the Indian village, and was so impressed by the beauty of one of the young Sioux women that he mentioned her by her name, Ampetu-Washtoy (meaning "Beautiful Day") in his *Memoirs* written nearly half a century later.

After replenishing supplies and making necessary repairs, the expedition pushed on, up the Minnesota River a hundred and fifteen miles to Big Swan Lake, about seventy-five miles southwest of Fort Snelling in an area later named Nicollet County after the leader of the expedition. Since an Indian tribe called the Sissiton

Sioux made their summer encampment there, Frémont had further opportunity to indulge in one of his favorite occupations: making friends with American Indians and studying their customs.

A little over a hundred miles farther southwest, near what is now the western boundary of Minnesota, they visited the red pipestone quarries. These are now a part of Pipestone National Monument in Pipestone County. Here a vein of workable red rock furnished the Indians with material out of which they carved their pipes and religious and ornamental figures. The vein of rock, also called Catlinite, after George Catlin who discovered it in 1836, was overlaid with sandstone. As the expedition, accompanied by friendly Indians, neared the quarry a severe volley of thunder roared overhead, a blaze of lightning lit the darkening sky, and a heavy rain poured on the group. Frémont noticed that the Indians made delighted signs to each other. Always curious, he asked why they were so pleased, and learned that the event was a confirmation of the Indian belief that, whenever a visitor approached the quarry, the spirit of the pipestone spoke its welcome in thunder and lightning.

This sort of welcome seemed to call for an acknowledgment, so the members of the expedition helped the Indians by blasting out some of the stone with gunpowder. For three days the white men and Indians visited each other in friendly companionship, and then the Nicollet expedition turned northward, over a prairie plateau 1,500 feet above sea level.

About a hundred miles farther north they came to

the finger-like Lac qui Parle—actually a widening of the Minnesota River in what is now Chippewa County—where they camped at the fortified trading post of Joseph Renville, a half-breed who was one of the ablest and most successful fur traders in the region. From him, as from Henry Sibley, Frémont learned a great deal about the Indians and how to get on with them harmoniously.

The 1837 exploration ended with a great hunting trip under the guidance of Henry Sibley and Jean Baptiste Faribault, another experienced fur trader. Accompanying them were all the Sioux Indians of a village, under Chief Red Dog. In the Iowa hunting grounds they spent several days shooting deer and elk, which furnished them with great feasts at night. Frémont was never to forget this trip, or, as he wrote in his *Memoirs*, the ". . . bright fires, where fat venison was roasting on sticks . . . or stewing with corn or wild rice in pots hanging from tripods; squaws busy over the cooking, and children rolling about the ground. No sleep is better or more restoring than follows such a dinner, earned by such a day."

One night the camp was awakened from sleep by the roar and glare of a prairie fire, and the party had barely time to set a back fire and get their animals out of danger before the blaze swept past them. On another day a squaw fell behind, only to catch up with them a few hours later carrying a newborn baby.

The winter was spent in St. Louis preparing for the 1839 expedition which was to carry them up the Missouri River, and in Washington, where their mass of carefully made notes and calculations was transferred to maps. Now Washington was far from dull, for there was a job to do. The remembered excitement that had come to Frémont during his school days, as he pored over a book on astronomy, returned as the older and more experienced Nicollet taught him in greater detail how astronomical observations were used in map-making. He had learned in the field how to determine altitudes by reading the barometer and making standardized calculations, how to find latitude and longitude by observing the height of the sun or the polestar above the horizon, by making telescopic observations of the eclipses of the satellites of Jupiter, and the passage of other planets over the sun, and by making extremely complicated mathematical calculations.

Now he and Nicollet were engaged in the last step in the intricate process: converting these figures into meaningful lines on paper to make accurate and trustworthy maps of the regions that had been explored.

The winter passed quickly and, early in April 1839, the Nicollet-Frémont expedition left St. Louis on the steamboat *Antelope,* belonging to the American Fur Company, headed up the Missouri River. The ship was to be their headquarters as far as Fort Pierre. Across the river from the fort, nearly 1,300 miles from St. Louis, was the site on which Pierre, the capital of South Dakota, later was established. With them went a party that included five new members engaged during the winter. Among them was Etienne Provot, an experienced moun-

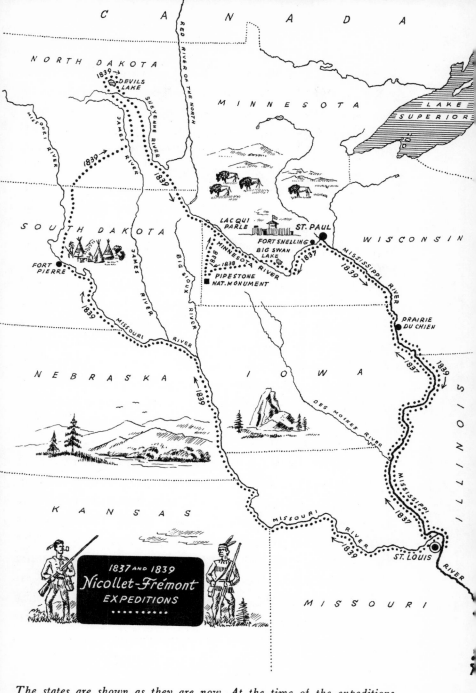

The states are shown as they are now. At the time of the expeditions, the only states in the area were Illinois, Michigan, and Missouri

taineer, after whom Provo, Utah, was later named, and Louis Zindel, a former Prussian artilleryman, expert in making rockets.

The voyage up the Missouri was a rough one. Shallow and swift, the river seemed constantly to be changing its channel, and often the boat would drag through sandbars, or be slowed by snags, and sometimes stand motionless against the swift current, with its keel embedded in the river bottom, head on into the current, while the captain maneuvered the helm to help it break loose. Then, with a roar, it would go on.

But there was plenty to occupy the attention of Nicollet and Frémont to keep them from being bored. As they pushed on and on upstream the intense stillness was more noticeable against the noisy exhaust of the *Antelope's* engine. Sometimes they ran through flat land in which the river spread out into several channels, and the captain had to make a hard decision as to which was the deepest. Sometimes they proceeded between majestic high wooded banks.

Often the noise of the engine would disturb turkey buzzards feasting on the dead carcass of a buffalo along the bank, and the birds would soar upward and sail in circles on their great wings, which remained motionless, waiting for the nuisance to pass. In the woods there were often vast flocks of migratory wild pigeons, which would rise on whistling wings in flocks so dense as to cloud the sunlight. Meanwhile Nicollet and Frémont kept happily busy charting the twisting and turning of the river.

On the seventieth day they reached Fort Pierre, the

principal post of the American Fur Company on the Missouri. They were now in the heart of the wild country dominated by Indians and buffalo. A large village of Yankton Sioux Indians stood within a few miles of the fort, and Nicollet visited it at once, carrying gifts for the chiefs that would insure the safe passage of the expedition through their territory.

Horse carts and provisions were obtained at the fort, and six men were added to the party, including William Dixon and Louison Frenière, interpreters and guides. Frenière was a half-breed with a widespread reputation as a buffalo hunter. C697291 ꚩꚩ. SCHOOꝆꙗ

When the expedition was ferried across to the eastern shore of the river, it consisted of 19 men, 33 horses, and 10 carts loaded with stores. Their course now lay eastward over flat land nearly two thousand feet above sea level, and five hundred feet above the river.

Frémont enjoyed riding beside Frenière and watching him as, with unerring skill, he would quickly identify specks on the horizon as antelopes, buffalo, white men, or Indians. He was never to forget the day when, for the first time, he heard the shout of "La vache! La vache!" (Buffalo!) from the hunters. In a moment the hunting horses were saddled and the hunters mounted, each carrying a gun and each with a handkerchief wound about his head. The herd of buffalo was moving down to drink at the edge of the river near which the camp was located: enormous old bulls with ragged hair hanging in patches, and lean cows anxiously watching the frolicking of calves.

As soon as the hunters were over the hill the buffalo saw them.

Frémont wrote in his *Memoirs:*

There was a sudden halt, a confused wavering movement, and then a headlong rout; the hunters in their midst. How I got down that . . . hillside I never knew. From the moment I saw the herd I never saw the ground again until all was over. I remember, as the charge was made, seeing the bulls in the rear turn, then take a few bounds forward, and then, turning for a last look, join the headlong flight.

As they broke into the herd the hunters separated. . . . But the only things visible to me in our flying course were the buffalo and the dust, and there was tumult in my breast as well as around me. I made repeated ineffectual attempts to steady myself for a shot at a cow after a hard struggle to get up with her, and each time barely escaped a fall. In such work a man must be able to forget his horse, but my horsemanship was not yet equal to such a proof. At the outset, when the hunters had searched over the herd and singled out each his fattest cow, and made a dash upon her, the herd broke into bands which spread over the plain. I clung to that where I found myself, unwilling to give up, until I found that neither horse nor man could bear the strain longer. Our furious speed had carried us far out over the prairies. Only some straggling groups were in sight, loping slowly off, seemingly conscious that the chase was over. I dismounted and reloaded, and sat down on the grass for a while to give us both rest.

Frémont did not realize at first that he was actually

Buffalo hunt

lost. Then slowly he was aware that not one of his companions was in sight, and that he had no idea where the camp was, save that it was somewhere south of him. The sun was low, and, wanting to get back to the others as quickly as he could, he decided to ride directly west, thinking he would reach the river while it was still daylight, and that he could then follow it back to camp. Some time after dark he came to a trail. Surely this would lead him somewhere. Out of pity for his weary horse, he got off and walked, bridle rein in hand. He had not gone far when he saw buffalo droppings and knew that he was following a buffalo trail that might lead anywhere.

Thoroughly discouraged, and convinced that he could not find his way back to camp that night, he went on only until he found fresh water at the bottom of a wooded ravine. After refreshing himself with a drink, and making several trips up the bank to carry water to his horse in his hat, he unsaddled the horse, put the saddle on the ground for a pillow, and lay down. As he did so, he noticed, to the south, a rocket soaring into the sky. Good old Zindel and his rockets! Another followed, and another, and Frémont knew that they were being sent up from the camp to show him where it was. He judged that he was about fifteen miles away from it, and, feeling that his tired horse and he could not find it in the dark, he lay down again to sleep, first putting his gun beside him, its barrel pointed directly toward where the rocket had gone up. The next day, following the direction indicated by the gun barrel, walking and leading

Lost on the prairie

his horse, he arrived at camp about noon, and the relieved party quickly started on.

Dixon guided the group over steep hills, bright with
flowers, and along the shores of small lakes into the
region between the James and Sheyenne rivers in what
is now North Dakota. Here, for three days, they found
themselves constantly surrounded by interminable herds
of buffalo. The great animals tramped along beside the
expedition, bellowing, raising huge clouds of dust, and
bringing with them hordes of flies. Then they fell in with
an encampment of some two thousand Sioux Indians and
learned that they had encountered a "grand surround"
of buffalo, in which the Indians gathered meat for the
winter.

Respecting the importance of the event to the Indians, Nicollet and Frémont asked when and by what
route they might pass in such a way as not to interfere
with the hunt. The hospitable Sioux, grateful to the
white men for their consideration, invited them to join
them and to dine at the lodges of the chiefs.

In return Nicollet and Frémont invited the chiefs to
a feast, and served a stew of fat buffalo meat and rice,
into which they had put some Swiss cheese as flavoring.
Frémont wrote in his *Memoirs:*

No one would begin until all the plates were filled. . . .
With the first mouthful each Indian silently laid down his
spoon, and each looked at the other. After a pause of be-
wilderment the interpreter succeeded in having the situation

understood. . . . Until this strange flavor was accounted for the Indians thought they were being poisoned; but, the cheese being shown to them, and explanation made, confidence was restored; and by the aid of several kettles of water well sweetened with molasses, . . . the dinner party went on . . . in great good humor and general satisfaction.

The white men watched the buffalo hunt with the excitement that superb horsemanship gives to any horse lover. Each Indian and his horse moved as one with a grace and rhythm that was like dancing. It has been said that an Indian on horseback could drive an eighteen-inch arrow with such force that it would pass through the animal and emerge on the other side. Indeed, one great Indian chief was said to have killed two buffalo with one arrow, which passed through the first animal and mortally wounded the second that was running alongside.

When the hunt was over, the Indians cut the buffalo meat into strips and hung it over scaffolding to be dried in the sun.

Several days later, when the Nicollet party reached the salty Devils Lake in northeastern North Dakota, they found traces of another large hunting party composed of *Bois-Brulés*—half-breed descendants of French, English, and Scotch, crossed with Chippewas, Sioux, and other Indian tribes. Each year they came down from Canada, where the supply of buffalo was becoming more and more scarce. They dried the meat in the sun or over fires and made it into pemmican—meat pounded into a coarse, fibrous mass, mixed with fat, and pressed into cakes, or packed into skin sacks—and hauled it home on carts.

After about a week spent in surveying Devils Lake, the expedition turned eastward and traveled across the Dakota Plateau, exploring and noting the headwaters of tributaries through prairie land ablaze with wild purple asters and goldenrod. From here, traveling southward, they recrossed the Sheyenne River on August 14, and some days later reached the Renville home again.

The party spent a few pleasant days with the Renvilles at Lac qui Parle. Then they descended the Minnesota River to the Mississippi and started down that river.

Early in November, Frémont, in a bark canoe with a detachment of the party, reached Prairie du Chien, Wisconsin. A steamboat was in dock there, preparing to leave for St. Louis, but Frémont thought it would be pleasant to rest a few days and take the next boat. In the morning, after the boat had left, he looked out of the window of the hotel into a blinding snowstorm, and learned that the river had frozen over from bank to bank during the night. The next boat would leave the following spring! His only recourse was to hire a wagon in which to make the long and tiring journey to St. Louis, from which he made his way to Washington.

Of the time lost in Prairie du Chien, he later wrote in his *Memoirs:* "I had time enough while there to learn two things: one, how to skate; the other, the value of a day."

Jessie

✠

HE JOHN CHARLES FRÉMONT who went to Washington after the Missouri River expedition was not the untried, little-known, young man who had gone there such a short time before to receive his commission as second lieutenant. Now he had been hardened by two years of strenuous experience in the field, had gained priceless technical knowledge, and had achieved great dignity.

After a visit to President Van Buren and Poinsett, during which the young man listened with modest pleasure to Nicollet's praise of him and the President's hearty congratulations, Nicollet and Frémont took a holiday in Baltimore visiting with friends of the noted Frenchman. While they were there Frémont learned of the death of his brother and hastened to Charleston to comfort his aging mother, whose pride in the accomplishments of her older son helped to assuage her grief over the death of the younger. In a few days, Frémont hurried back to Washington to begin, with Nicollet, the long careful work of map-making.

The two men had living quarters together in the

house of a bachelor friend of Nicollet, a gifted scientist named Ferdinand Hassler, Superintendent of the Coast Survey, who was well known to Washington society. Some of their work of map-making was done here, and some in an office of the nearby Survey Building. An observatory was built on the top of Mr. Hassler's house and, at night, Frémont and Nicollet often watched the stars and made astronomical calculations.

Many men prominent in the government came to watch the map-makers at work in the Survey Building. Among them was Senator Thomas Hart Benton from Missouri. Frémont and Nicollet were often invited guests at Senator Benton's home, where they met other senators who, like Benton, were deeply interested in the opening and settlement of the West—the vast region between the Mississippi and the Pacific Ocean. They wanted not only to protect the claims of the United States on the western coast, but also to establish a Pacific port for its naval vessels, to protect the fur trade, and to provide overland communication between the East and the West. Benton was especially interested in seeing the Columbia River region settled and having his country's claim to it enforced. Nicollet was now in poor health, and more and more Benton talked over his plans for an overland expedition beyond the Missouri with Frémont, until it became at least tacitly understood that the younger man would lead the expedition when it became a reality.

But before that time there were other events of great importance to the young Frémont.

Thomas Hart Benton

There were five children in the Benton family—four girls and a boy. The two oldest daughters, Sarah and Jessie, were at Miss English's boarding school at Georgetown, three miles away; the two younger sisters, and the brother, Randolph, were at home. Frémont had made friends with the children at home, in the casual way that a warm-hearted young man will make friends with children, but when the senator and Mrs. Benton took him to a concert at Miss English's school and he met Jessie, his reaction to her was not that of simple friendship. She was still not sixteen years old; yet she was unusually womanly, both physically and mentally, with her brown hair and eyes, her delightful oval face, her sparkling good humor, and her excellent mind. Frémont had always been susceptible to a beautiful young woman, but his feeling about Jessie was far from a mere passing attraction. He apparently knew instinctively and at once that this one was the woman with whom he wanted to spend the rest of his life. "There came a glow in my heart," Frémont wrote of the meeting later, "which changed the current and color of daily life and gave a beauty to common things."

Jessie was apparently equally attracted to Frémont's lean handsomeness and his impetuousness. But it was not until she had returned home for a vacation several months later that the two young people could see each other frequently. Then Frémont was a constant visitor at the Benton house.

Soon the elder Bentons, seeing how things were going, took a hand. They admired Frémont, and were fond of him, but Jessie was so young, and Frémont's salary as an army officer so small! The crisis came on the day of President William Harrison's funeral, a month after his having taken office. Nicollet and Frémont had invited the Bentons to their quarters in the Hassler house, from the windows of which there was a fine view of the impressive funeral parade. But while the others watched, Frémont and Jessie seemed completely occupied with each other, and the glow in the faces of both of them clearly betrayed where their interests were.

The next day Mrs. Benton had a long talk with her friend Mrs. Poinsett, and asked for her help. Mrs. Poinsett talked to her husband, the Secretary of War, and Frémont was astounded when he was suddenly ordered away from his task of making maps with Nicollet to make a survey of the Des Moines River in Iowa Territory. In vain Nicollet protested at losing his most valuable assistant; Poinsett was adamant. As Frémont left for Iowa Territory, Jessie was taken off to Virginia to members of her mother's family. It was a blow to both lovers; yet they were not left without hope. It was understood that, if they would stay apart for a year, and if at the end of that time their feelings had not changed, there would be no further opposition to their marriage.

But Jessie's parents were to be disappointed. A letter from Nicollet to Frémont must have added to the young man's impetuous haste to finish his work, get back to Washington, and claim his bride.

"Everyone here and in Baltimore," the Frenchman wrote, "inquires after you; even the Benton Household, every time I go there. The young girls returned home evening before last. . . . Everything is going well; she is quite happy, and she is impatient to see you."

Jessie was now a little over seventeen, felt herself a woman rather than a girl, and knew her own mind. Undoubtedly she had decided, even before Frémont returned from his Iowa survey, just what they would do, and had kept her own council about it.

Less than six months after leaving Washington, Frémont was back with the geographic and astronomical notes that he had made in the field. For a time he was busy, transferring his data to maps. He saw Jessie as often as possible, against the continued opposition of her parents. Indeed they seemed more strongly opposed to the marriage than ever, and the two young people began to fear that, even if they waited until the year was up, Senator and Mrs. Benton would still oppose their marriage. Then why wait?

Secretly they went from one clergyman to another in Washington, asking each to marry them. Each one told them that he would be glad to, if the seventeen-and-a-half-year-old Jessie could get her parents' consent, but that otherwise he could not. Finally an older friend of Jessie, who was in sympathy with their desire, prevailed upon a clergyman friend to perform the ceremony and, on October 19, 1841, they were married.

For some time they kept the marriage secret, seeing each other when they could, but finally Frémont summoned up all of his courage, and together they went to Senator Benton to whom Frémont haltingly blurted out the news. In a flaming rage, Benton ordered his son-in-law to leave the house and never return, adding that Jessie would stay at home. But he had reckoned without the determination of his daughter, who promptly took her husband's arm and announced that wherever he went she would go. This crumpled the angry senator's last defense, and, instead of leaving the house, Frémont moved in. The hatchet was buried, and Senator Benton gave the cooperative support that was to make many of Frémont's later accomplishments possible.

Through the South Pass
to Frémont's Peak

☩

ICOLLET had been ill, in Baltimore, for some months. He still worked feverishly on his report of the Missouri River exploration, but it was increasingly clear that he would not be able to lead the expedition to the West that had been planned for the following year. The decision became definite on New Year's day, 1842.

The young Frémonts made a ceremonial call on President Tyler, shook hands, not only with the President but also with such dignitaries as John Calhoun, Daniel Webster, and Winfield Scott, and wished all a happy new year. Then they went to the Benton house, where Jessie helped to receive guests. Here Senator Benton and others discussed the matter and decided that Frémont, not Nicollet, must lead the expedition.

Thus it was that, on May 2, 1842, Frémont, not quite seven months after his marriage to Jessie, left her in Washington and again turned his face westward. There is every reason to believe that he regretted leaving his bride for so long a trip. But it seems equally certain that his regret was tempered by his joy at starting out in charge of his own expedition. He was only twenty-nine years old, and could justifiably take pride in having been given such an important assignment. The objectives of this first expedition were limited. He was to go only as far as the South Pass of the Rockies, about eighty miles southwest of the center of what is now Wyoming. And even South Pass was an addition on which Frémont himself insisted.

The route had been traveled before, notably in 1824 by Jedidiah Smith and Thomas Fitzpatrick. Six years later Smith, in partnership with William Sublette and David E. Jackson, conducted the first expedition to include wagons, from St. Louis to the mountains. The party consisted of eighty men mounted on mules; ten wagons, each drawn by five mules; and two light four-wheeled carriages called dearborns, each drawn by a single mule. Others also made the trip. Thus the famous Oregon Trail was established.

Actually it was not quite a stable and fixed route, but varied somewhat according to the judgment of the early travelers. The route, with its variations, was well known to those who had traveled it, and to western guides, but it had never been accurately mapped. It was this important task that had now been assigned to Frémont. His twelve-year-old brother-in-law, Randolph Benton, was with him, because his parents felt that a few months spent on an expedition with Frémont would broaden and toughen the lad.

Frémont and Randolph traveled from Washington to Baltimore by the newly built railroad, and from there by a succession of stagecoaches and boats, the journey ending with a magnificently scenic trip by steamboat from Cincinnati down the Ohio and the Mississippi. Lumber rafts, keelboats transporting merchandise, skiffs, and floating logs crowded the mighty river.

Twenty days after leaving Washington the travelers reached St. Louis, and went at once to the home of Mrs. Sarah Benton Brant, the favorite niece of Jessie's mother, whose guests they were to be while Frémont was arranging for the house of Chouteau to equip the expedition.

When arrangements were completed in St. Louis, Frémont boarded a steamboat on the Missouri that would take him to Kansas Landing, near what is now Kansas City. From there he would go on to Chouteau's Post. With him, of course, was Randolph and, at St. Louis, another junior member had been added to the party: Henry Brant, the nineteen-year-old son of his St. Louis hostess. Henry was to act as a sort of general aide and chore boy.

As the little steamer ploughed its way up the turbulent Missouri, a memorable meeting occurred on board. A fellow passenger was a man who has come down in history as the hero of every schoolboy, a mountain man beyond compare, a courageous buffalo hunter and Indian fighter, and an all-round romantic figure of the Far West—the bold yet gentle Kit Carson. His knowledge of the western rivers and mountain passes was phenomenal.

Four years older than Frémont, Kit was a son of

Kentucky and spoke with the slow soft drawl of the South. At fifteen he had left home to enjoy the wild free life of the West, and had been living as a frontiersman ever since. He had indomitable courage, but was a man of peace, and avoided quarrels as long as possible. When fighting became unavoidable, he was a foe to be reckoned with by the most skillful and courageous. There were many stories about him. One that Carson himself liked, though he never boasted about it, told how he had happened to meet a man named Shunar, who, he knew, had threatened to kill him on sight. Kit quietly rode up to Shunar and asked him whether he was looking for someone. Shunar answered no, but, as he spoke, lifted his rifle and aimed it at Kit's heart. Before he could fire, however, Kit had discharged his own pistol from his belt, shattering Shunar's wrist and deflecting the rifle's bullet, which merely scorched Kit's forehead. Another man might have shot to kill and felt justified in so doing. Kit used his ability to act quickly and his superb marksmanship only to save his own life, not to take another's.

He was a man of uncompromising integrity and reliability. Six years after Carson and Frémont met, the latter wrote of him, "With me, Carson and Truth mean the same thing."

Kit's method of preparing for any eventuality at night in camp was described in an article in *Harper's Magazine* for August 1853. His saddle, which he used as a pillow, was always arranged so that it formed a barricade to protect his head. He placed two pistols, half cocked, above it, always in exactly the same place so that he could lay his hands on them without thinking. He put his rifle beneath his blanket at his side, within quick reach, and also where it would not get damp. During the evening he customarily kept out of the glare of the campfire, and when he had to come near it to light his pipe, he did it rapidly, exposing himself as little as possible.

While still quite young Kit had married an Indian girl to whom he was devoted. Shortly after having borne one child, a daughter, she died. Now Kit found some comfort in devoting himself to his daughter. When she was of a suitable age he sent her to St. Louis that she might be properly educated. At the time of his meeting with Frémont he was returning from an unaccustomed trip to the scenes of his childhood, which had ended by a visit with his daughter in St. Louis.

Frémont's meeting with Carson, as they journeyed up the Missouri in 1842, was especially fortunate for both of them, and marked the beginning of a partnership based on friendship and mutual trust which was to last until Carson's death in 1868. Each instinctively recognized the qualities of the other at once and, when Frémont offered Carson a position as guide of the expedition at a salary of $100 a month, Kit accepted it without hesitation.

At Chouteau's Post, while the expedition was preparing to get under way, Carson sent two Delaware Indian runners along the Santa Fe Trail to Taos, to ask fifteen men, who had worked closely with him before, to equip themselves and meet the expedition at Fort Laramie.

It was not Carson's or Frémont's intention to have these men join the expedition. Kit had asked them to come to Fort Laramie and hunt and trap in the general vicinity of the Frémont party in order to have them nearby in case of trouble with the Indians. Throughout the summer they could have been reached quickly enough by a messenger to come to the aid of the Frémont expedition if needed.

On June 10, the expedition left Chouteau's Post and started on its long trek. As the column passed out of the belt of woods near the Post it consisted of Frémont; Kit Carson; Randolph Benton; Henry Brant; Charles Preuss, a friend of Frémont, who would act as topographer; Lucien Maxwell, engaged as a hunter who was to keep the party supplied with fresh meat; and nineteen voyageurs, most of whom were French Creoles, and all of whom were armed. Eleven of these were mounted on excellent horses. The other eight drove mule carts carrying baggage, food, and scientific equipment. Eight oxen, which would be slaughtered if buffalo meat became scarce, and several spare horses made up the rest of the column.

The plan for the expedition was to proceed first up the valley of the Kansas River, where Frémont was to observe and note its general character and plot it, then to turn north and go to the Platte River, which they would follow to the west.

Soon they found themselves in the midst of an enormous herd of buffalo. Frémont wrote later:

In the sight of such a mass of life, the traveler feels a strange emotion of grandeur. We had heard from a distance a dull and confused murmuring, and when we came in view of their dark masses, there was not one among us who did not feel his heart beat quicker. It was the early part of the day, when the herds are feeding; and everywhere they were in motion. Here and there a huge old bull was rolling in the grass, and clouds of dust rose in the air from various parts of the bands, each the scene of some obstinate fight. Indians and buffalo make the poetry and life of the prairie, and our camp was full of their exhilaration.

For several days they were in the midst of buffalo, and feasted on roast meat. One day Kit's horse fell headlong, throwing its rider, then got up and raced after the band of buffalo, to be caught only with difficulty later by Maxwell. At another time one of the mules, apparently deciding that the life of the prairie was a good one, broke away from camp and left with a herd of buffalo. Though several men were sent in pursuit, the mule was not recovered.

The routine of camp and trail life varied little from day to day, save as conditions of the land over which the expedition traveled made necessary. At daylight the camp was aroused, the animals turned loose to graze, and breakfast was eaten at about six o'clock. Immediately after breakfast the march was resumed. At noon there was a halt of one or two hours, and the march then continued until within about an hour of sunset, when camp was made. Actually they spent the night in an improvised fortified post, rather than a mere camp. Before sunset the wagons were wheeled into a compact circle, forming an effective barricade. Within this fortified circle the tents were pitched and fire made. The horses and mules were hobbled and turned loose to graze, but when darkness fell they were gathered close to the wagons and tethered with twenty- or thirty-foot ropes. Three sentries were set and changed at two-hour intervals during the night.

When the expedition reached Fort Laramie it received alarming news. Jim Bridger, one of the most famous of fur traders and mountain men, was there, having just come down the North Platte River. He reported that three large Indian tribes—the Sioux, the Blackfeet, and the Cheyenne—had joined forces and were on the warpath, sworn to kill all white men they met in order to avenge the death of a number of Sioux at the hands of a party of trappers and Snake Indians. Several trappers and friendly Indians in the Fort soberly warned Frémont against continuing his march, at least until the war parties had returned to their homes. All of the voyageurs in the Frémont party were alarmed, and even Kit Carson viewed the prospect so seriously that he made a will. But Frémont was adamant. He had insisted that the plans for the expedition include a survey of South Pass, and to South Pass he would go. Further, he knew that there was a party of emigrants to Oregon just ahead who might need protection. He did, however, insist on leaving Ran-

Fort Laramie

dolph Benton and Henry Brant in the fort, feeling that he would not be justified in subjecting them to the danger Bridger had reported.

Before they left, Frémont was invited to a dog feast by one of the Indian chiefs. Dog meat was considered a great delicacy, and a guest to whom it was served was honored. Reluctantly Frémont, who liked dogs in their living state too well to enjoy the thought of eating one, accepted. He wrote later:

. . . the women and children were sitting outside the lodge, and we took our seats on buffalo robes spread around. The dog was in a large pot over the fire, in the middle of the lodge, and immediately on our arrival was dished up in large wooden bowls, one of which was handed to each. . . . Feeling something move behind me, I looked round, and found that I had taken my seat among a litter of fat young puppies. . . . fortunately, I am not of delicate nerves, and continued quietly to empty my platter.

Probably no other event in the early partnership of Frémont and Carson so impressed Carson as Frémont's decision to go on in the face of probable danger. Here was a man after his own heart, one who was not deterred from his plans and his duty by the prospect of fighting. Inwardly he must have cheered his companion. And at the same time he probably thought with comfort of the party of fifteen of his old supporters who would be near enough to be called on for help if help were needed.

Fortunately, it was not. After leaving Fort Laramie on

July 19 the expedition proceeded peacefully onward, at no point meeting any unfriendly Indians. On August 8 they reached South Pass, the principal objective of the expedition. But still they pushed on, Frémont wanting to explore the Wind River chain of mountains, the highest in Wyoming. Here they found what Frémont believed (wrongly as it was later to be discovered) to be the highest peak in the range.

He was determined to climb it. But before he could do so an accident delayed his further movements. The expedition was fording a stream, over many boulders that were always slippery and sometimes not clearly visible. The pack animals fell repeatedly. As a result of one of these falls, the only barometer that Frémont had with him struck a rock and broke. Without it he would be unable to measure the altitude of the peak he was about to climb, or any other elevation.

To the men the accident seemed an obstacle that could not be overcome. But no sooner had they settled into camp than Frémont began to study the situation and attempt to remedy it. He found that the glass cistern had been broken, but that the tube was undamaged and that no air had entered it. Therefore, he reasoned, if he could successfully replace the cistern, all would be well. He tried to use each of a number of glass bottles that he had, and spent an entire day cutting them, one after another, to the right size, with a rough file. But each of them broke in the wrong place. The next day he changed his plan. Finding a powder horn that was exceptionally translucent, he boiled it, stretched it in order to make it the correct diameter, scraped it very thin to make it even more translucent, cut it to size, fastened it in place with glue made from a buffalo's tendons, and filled it with mercury. After the glue had dried, the barometer was tested. It recorded almost the identical readings they had gotten from it before it was broken.

Both men and animals were by now feeling the poison of deep fatigue. Their food consisted of tasteless, dried buffalo meat. They had fulfilled the mission that had been assigned to them, and most of them wanted only to get back to the creature comforts of civilization.

But to Frémont, leaving the scene of this mighty peak without reaching its top was unthinkable. Quickly he made his plans. Large oak trees were felled to form a breastwork about the camp against possible attack by the Blackfeet Indians. A party was left here on guard while Frémont, with fourteen men, including Kit Carson, left on the twelfth of August to make the hazardous climb to the top of the peak. On the fourteenth, some of the party had, with great difficulty, reached a spot at which Frémont stopped to consider whether the satisfaction of reaching the top was worth the arduous effort it would take. Finally he decided that he would make one more attempt, but that he would take only those men who volunteered to accompany him. On the fifteenth, he sent a number of them back under Kit Carson and continued his climb with five companions. After some climbing, so rough that it would have turned many back, they found themselves confronted with a perpendicular wall. Getting toe- and finger-holds where they could, they climbed it slowly. At the snow line they put on light buffalo-skin moccasins, which made it possible to use their toes more effectively, and continued. Soon Frémont, who was in the lead, found that, in order to proceed farther, he must work his way along a vertical precipice by clinging to the crevices. But once across, it would be an easy matter to reach the top.

"I sprang upon the summit," he wrote later, "and another step would have precipitated me into an immense snow field five hundred feet below. To the edge of this field was a sheer icy precipice."

John Charles Frémont was to know many moments of deep elation during his busy and eventful life, but it is doubtful whether any moved him more than his conquest of the peak that now bears his name. And something happened there that most men would not have noticed, but that, to Frémont, was a fine adventure. He wrote:

A stillness the most profound and a terrible solitude forced themselves constantly on the mind as the great features of the place. Here, on the summit, where the stillness was absolute, unbroken by any sound, and the solitude complete, we thought ourselves beyond the region of animated life; but, while we were sitting on the rock, a solitary bee (*bromus,* the humble bee) came winging his flight from the eastern valley and lit on the knee of one of the men. It was a strange place, the icy rock and the highest peak of the Rocky Mountains, for a lover of warm sunshine and flowers; and we pleased ourselves with the idea that he was

*Frémont plants the American flag on the high peak
of the Rocky Mountains*

the first of his species to cross the mountain barrier—a solitary pioneer to foretell the advance of civilization.

After fixing a ramrod into a small crevice in the rock
that formed the summit, Frémont attached a flag he had
brought with him. It had the thirteen stripes of the flag

of the United States, but in the corner, where the field of stars is usually placed, there was a white field bearing a blue eagle resting on a peace pipe, and blue stars. Before he left the peak he took up the flag again and carried it home, and it later served a rather special purpose, as we shall see.

The plans for the expedition called for a survey of the Platte River. So, in order to get home as quickly as possible and, at the same time, carry out the waterway survey, Frémont decided to cover as much of the journey as he could by boat. The Sweetwater, which the expedition followed to its junction with the Platte, was too shallow for navigation, but when they got to the Platte they found it deep and swift. Therefore, he had his men inflate their collapsible rubber boat and launch it. He then divided them into two parties. One of these, led by Frémont, would use the boat; the other would go overland to Goat Island in the Platte and meet the boat party there.

Frémont's own graphic account in his *Memoirs* tells the story of that mad and disastrous dash down the Platte River:

We started before sunrise, intending to breakfast at Goat Island. . . . Preuss accompanied me, and with us were five of my best men, . . . Here appeared no scarcity of water, and we took on board, with various instruments and baggage, provisions for ten or twelve days. We paddled down the river rapidly, for our little craft was light as a duck on the water; and the sun had been some time risen, when we heard before us a hollow roar, which we supposed to be that of a fall. . . .

. . . we passed three cataracts in succession, . . . We were so delighted with the performance of our boat, and so confident in her powers, that we would not have hesitated to leap a fall of ten feet with her. We put to shore for breakfast . . . for it was now eight o'clock, and we had been working since daylight, and were all wet, fatigued, and hungry. . . .

We re-embarked at nine o'clock, and in about twenty minutes reached the next cañon. . . . It was simply a narrow, dark chasm in the rock; and here the perpendicular faces were . . . two to three hundred, and farther down, as we afterward ascertained, five hundred feet in vertical height. Our previous success had made us bold, and we determined again to run the cañon. Everything was secured as firmly as possible; and, having divested ourselves of the greater part of our clothing, we pushed into the stream. . . .

An ugly pass lay before us. We had made fast to the stern of the boat a strong rope about fifty feet long; and three of the men clambered along among the rocks, and with this rope let her down slowly through the pass. . . . in the narrows it required all our strength and skill to avoid staving the boat on the sharp points. In one of these the boat . . . stuck fast for an instant . . . The water swept overboard . . . a sextant and a pair of saddlebags. I caught the sextant as it passed by me; but the saddlebags became the prey of the whirlpools. . . . after making a little distance the force of the current became too great for the men on shore, and two of them let go the rope. [Basil] Lajeunesse, the third man, hung on, and was jerked head-foremost into

the river from a rock about twelve feet high; and down the
boat shot like an arrow, Basil following us in the rapid current and exerting all of his strength to keep in mid-channel
—his head only seen occasionally like a black spot in the
white foam.

As soon as possible the men turned the boat into an

*The perilous passage through the canyon
in the Platte River*

eddy, and soon the black head of Lajeunesse came bobbing up beside them, commenting calmly in French on the distance he had swum. Taking him and the two men who had followed on shore aboard, the men continued the rapid journey.

Frémont went on:

We cleared rock after rock, and shot past fall after fall, our little boat seeming to play with the cataract. We became flushed with success and familiar with the danger; and, yielding to the excitement of the occasion, broke forth together into a Canadian boat song. Singing, or rather shouting, we dashed along; and were, I believe, in the midst of the chorus, when the boat struck a concealed rock immediately at the foot of a fall, which whirled her over in an instant. Three of my men could not swim, and my first feeling was to assist them and save some of our effects; but a sharp concussion or two convinced me that I had not yet saved myself. A few strokes brought me into an eddy, and I landed on a pile of rocks on the left side. . . .

For a hundred yards below, the current was covered with floating books and boxes, bales of blankets, and scattered articles of clothing; and so strong and boiling was the stream that even our heavy instruments, which were all in cases, kept on the surface, . . .

Such was the disastrous end of that mad and joyous dash of Frémont and his singing boatmen down the Platte. Most of the more important records of the expedition were rescued from the river and preserved. But the arms and ammunition and all of the provisions were gone. Frémont had also lost one of his moccasins, so that his march over the rocky terrain with one bare foot became painful.

That evening they joined the other party at Goat Island. From there they proceeded to Fort Laramie. The record is not clear as to whether Kit Carson, his task as a guide finished, left the expedition here or had left it at the Wind River Range. It was the month of September 1842. The expedition had taken about three months.

On October 29, Frémont reached Washington, where, two weeks later (on November 13), Jessie bore their first child, a girl. Over his tiny daughter Frémont spread the wind-whipped flag that he had raised on Frémont's Peak, saying, "This flag was raised over the highest peak of the Rockies. I have brought it to you."

Frémont's happiness now seemed complete. He had just finished successfully an important surveying mission, and he had come back to his beautiful young wife in time to welcome joyously his first child. What more could a man of twenty-nine want?

They named the child Elizabeth Benton Frémont, but called her "Lilly," the name by which she was to be known throughout her life.

Jessie Defies the Army

✠

RÉMONT spent that winter of 1842–43 in Washington writing his report of the expedition with Jessie's help. Actually it was Jessie who did the writing, working from Frémont's dictation and improving the literary style as she went along. The result was Frémont's first book, a slim work of 120 pages which, after it was printed by order of Congress, came to be of great use to the increasing tide of travelers to the West.

The section of the report dealing with the region between the Missouri River and the Rocky Mountains was one of its most important parts. Major Stephen Long, after his expedition of 1819–20, had reported that the land in this area was "almost wholly unfit for cultivation, and of course uninhabitable by a people depending upon agriculture for their subsistence." Frémont's report corrected this error in no uncertain terms, and thus provided encouragement for the settlement of what later became the states of Nebraska, Kansas, and Oklahoma.

Meanwhile Senator Benton was using all of his influence to arrange for a second, and more ambitious, western expedition for Frémont. The plan this time included the finding of another route to South Pass, with a more favorable climate, and the region south of the Columbia River, between the Rockies and the Pacific Ocean, was to be explored and mapped.

Ever since Captain Gray of Boston sailed his ship *Columbia* to the West Coast in 1792, discovered the mouth of a great river and named it after his ship, the territory through which it flowed had been the subject of controversy between the United States and England. For Captain Gray had sailed into the river and this, according to a doctrine always practiced and enforced by the British, established claim to the territory drained by the river and its tributaries for the country of which the discoverer was a national. Yet the British were unwilling to relinquish all claim to the territory, even after John Jacob Astor and others had established a fur trading post at the mouth of the river and called it Astoria.

In 1818 Great Britain and the United States agreed that both nations should for ten years enjoy equally the privileges of all the bays and harbors on the coast. In 1827 the agreement was renewed for an indefinite period of time, but with the stipulation that either nation might cancel it by giving the other a year's notice. (It was actually not until 1846 that the matter was settled and clear title to the region taken by the United States.) Meanwhile the increasing interest in the Columbia Country and the continuous stream of immigrants to it, made it essential that as much as possible be known of the region. It was in response to this need that Frémont's second expedition was planned.

In March 1843, at the adjournment of Congress, Senator Benton hurried to St. Louis. Close behind him were Frémont, with Jessie, their baby, Mrs. Benton, Preuss—who was to accompany Frémont on the expedition—and a young free Negro named Jacob Dodson, eighteen years old, nearly six feet tall, and of exceptional strength. Members of his family had been servants in the Benton household from childhood, and there was mutual trust and affection between the Dodsons and the Bentons. Jacob had expressed a desire to go with Frémont, and the latter, seeing at once how useful the young man might be, quickly consented. Jacob proved his usefulness even before they reached St. Louis.

The party's coach was on a narrow road in the mountains of Pennsylvania, when a large wagon approached. The driver of the wagon shouted a warning that the road was too narrow for passing, and asked the coach driver to wait at one side, but the coachman paid no attention and drove on. As he tried to pass the wagon, the coach ran off the road, turned over, and came to rest on its roof, while the frightened horses began to plunge in panic. But just as the coach began to turn, Jacob leaped from the box where he was sitting, seized the horses' heads and, by a combination of strength and gentleness, calmed them before they had dashed the whole conveyance over the edge of the steep slope along which the road ran.

No one was injured but Mrs. Benton, who had received a painful blow on the head. Frémont thought it better for her to rest a day before going on. The entire party went to an old Pennsylvania tavern, which was near the place of the accident. Frémont was always to remember the abundance and excellence of the food: "buckwheat cakes half an inch thick and porous like a sponge, capable of absorbing enough of the good mountain butter to support a man for a day, with honey from the buckwheat fields, and maple syrup from the forest. The venison steaks were excellent, broiled over wood coals."

Two weeks later the party reached St. Louis and went to the Brant house to stay while Frémont made some arrangements in the city for his expedition. He bought some mules, and obtained a twelve-pound howitzer from Colonel S. W. Kearny, commander of the U.S. Army garrison at St. Louis. Frémont justified his request—or felt that he had justified it—by saying that he might need it against "Indians who had for many years a known character for audacious bravery and treachery." It was invented by the French for use in the mountains during their war with Algiers, and admirably suited to its purpose. He also engaged some of the men he would take with him, including Basil Lajeunesse and Louis Zindel, both of whom had been on the first expedition. Knowing that he would not be joined by Kit Carson until he had reached the Rocky Mountain country, he also engaged a new guide, Thomas Fitzpatrick, who had a reputation similar to that of Carson.

A brave man, well acquainted with the western trails, Fitzpatrick had once been in a fight with Blackfeet Indians, in which every member of his party except himself had been killed. He had hidden from the Indians in the rocks for three days, emerging only when they had given up the search and gone away. But the experience had left a lasting mark on him: though he was still a young man his hair was snow-white.

Then, with Preuss, the men he had hired, and the equipment and livestock he had obtained, Frémont went to Kansas Landing. Here the rapid increase in western transportation was apparent. Over a thousand travelers on the way to Oregon or California were pausing there, as was Frémont, to complete their preparations for the long trip overland. And more kept coming up the Missouri by steamboat. The little town was buzzing with activity, and swelling with a transient population which exceeded that of the permanent residents.

The Frémont expedition was almost ready to depart when two men arrived on horseback. One was DeRosier, who was to accompany the expedition but who had stayed behind in St. Louis because his wife was ill. He had made the trip to deliver a letter from Frémont's wife which Jessie wanted her husband to receive as quickly as possible. DeRosier's brother had come along to take Frémont's answer back. Frémont opened the envelope eagerly, though with some fear that it might bring bad news of Jessie or the baby. It contained only a short message urging him to leave for the West without delay, going immediately to Bent's Fort. There was no explanation.

Instantly he sat down and wrote hastily, "Good bye. I trust and go," and sent the letter back by DeRosier's brother. Early the next morning the men, animals, and whatever equipment was ready left Kansas Landing and traveled four miles, where camp was made on the prairie for one day while final details were worked out. When the expedition got truly under way the next day, May 30, 1843, it consisted of Frémont and 39 men. Each carried a Hall's carbine and a pistol. Two Delaware Indians—a young man and his father—went along as hunters.

A dozen large carts were drawn by two mules each, and a covered wagon carried the excellent refracting telescope, two fine chronometers, two sextants, two different kinds of barometers, several thermometers and compasses, and other scientific instruments. There were tents, a large supply of gifts for the Indians, a rubber boat, ample provisions, and the howitzer Frémont had obtained in St. Louis.

It was the howitzer that had brought about Jessie's urgent message. Later Frémont learned that she had opened a letter addressed to him from the Topographical Corps and read with consternation an order from Colonel J. J. Abert demanding that Frémont return to Washington at once and explain why he was taking a howitzer with him. Meanwhile, the letter went on, another officer would be sent to direct the expedition.

The message made Jessie's nineteen-year-old blood boil! She knew that, even if her husband were able to justify his act and return to his expedition, the time consumed by the trip to Washington, the slow questioning there, and his return would mean a delay of weeks, which would prevent him from doing all that he had planned to do before winter. So, without telling anyone, she wrote to her husband. She had not said more in her note in case it should happen to fall into other hands than her husband's. She knew that Frémont would trust her judgment, and that, once he had left Kansas Landing, there would be little likelihood of any other message reaching him until the matter had been adjusted. "You see," she wrote later, "I was afraid the order had been sent in duplicate and might, even with the detention from fogs and snags, yet overtake Mr. Frémont. It was in the blessed day before telegrams . . ."

After sending the message to her husband, Jessie wrote Colonel Abert telling him exactly what she had done, and why. Her father also wrote a letter, somewhat sterner than Jessie's, asking the colonel by what authority he had countermanded the orders to Frémont to set out on the expedition. The colonel did not reply to Jessie's letter or to the senator's, and no more was heard of the howitzer from Washington.

To Oregon

✠

THE EXPEDITION left the temporary camp
four miles from Kansas Landing on May 31, and
fell in with several emigrant parties. Their covered
wagons, drawn by oxen, or horses, or mules, were loaded
with furniture, farming utensils, provisions. Some had
chickens. Women with babies in their arms were in some
of the wagons. The men and the older children usually
walked. One of the wagons that the expedition met on
the first day out contained the complete equipment for a
mill which J. B. Childs of Missouri planned to set up on
the Sacramento River in California.

For three days the route of the first expedition was
followed. There were many more immigrant wagon
trains on the trail than there had been a year earlier.
Often the line of wagon trains stretched back as far as
the eye could see. The line would turn aside at a river
in order to cross at the best spot, or swerve to avoid an
abrupt rise in the land that would be difficult to climb.
The wagons' white tops, when they were not obscured
by clouds of dust, gleamed in the sunlight. The lowing
of oxen, the creaking of the wagons and harnesses, the

cries of the drivers, and the cracking of their whips filled the air with sound which seemed strangely out of place in the wide expanses of the grass-covered plain. Now and then a small party of Indians, or just one on horseback, would ride out onto the prairie, stop far enough away to be out of musket range, watch for a few minutes, then turn and gallop swiftly away. Those who traveled in large parties felt secure, knowing that an Indian attack was much less likely after a scout or scouting party had reported seeing a long wagon train.

On the third of June the Frémont party left the accustomed trail to follow the south bank of the Kansas River. This cut them off from the companionship and additional security of the wagon trains and made them dependent upon their own resources for protection. More than once they were aware of danger. Three days after they had left the trail, Maxwell, who had been out searching for a horse that had wandered away, came dashing into camp at a fast gallop. He was pursued by a war party of Osage Indians, wearing gay red blankets, their heads shaved except for scalp locks. When they saw the strength of the party of white men, the Indians did not linger. But they did speed their mounts through the camp, and skillfully make off with a number of Frémont's horses. Immediately, some members of the expedition followed them on swift mounts and, after a chase of seven or eight miles, returned with the stolen horses. The Indians had disappeared.

Now and then the members of the expedition saw herds of elk and antelope pause—usually just out of rifle range—to stare at the procession before turning and dashing away. Frequently they crossed prairie-dog villages where the horses had to step carefully to avoid stumbling in one of the little creatures' burrows. Frémont, ever curious, stopped in one of these villages and tried to dig one of its occupants out. But he was unsuccessful. He reported later in his *Memoirs* that the tunnel went down on a slant two feet, then turned and descended in a different direction another foot, then turned upward to join another hole. "I have no doubt," he added, "that all their little habitations communicate with each other." Thus they always had a ready means of escape.

After a brief delay occasioned by the need to make a raft for crossing the Smoky Hill River, the party went on, following the Republican River to the south fork of the Platte.

Here they surprised a grizzly bear taking a leisurely walk. Apparently astonished at the animals and men who had dared to intrude upon him, the huge creature stood on his hind legs, towering over the tallest man, displaying his tremendous size and strength for a moment, as he took a good look. Then, with a contemptuous snort, he dropped to the ground, turned, plunged into the river, swam to the other side, and walked calmly away.

A few days later the party met another bear, less peaceably inclined. He was digging for edible roots when they came upon him, but instead of showing his dislike for their interruption by leaving the scene, he charged them. Fired upon and wounded, he retreated

Kit Carson

to a rocky piny ridge, but when the mounted hunters
followed him, he charged again. A running fight between bear and hunters went on for some time, but
finally the valiant old fellow was brought down with six
bullets in him. By now the expedition was short of fresh
meat and would have been glad of an addition to their
scanty supply, but the poor old grizzly was so thin, that
he added nothing to the larder.

By now they were in sight of Pike's Peak, the most
conspicuous landmark in the Rockies. Though it was
early July, the mountain top was covered with snow that
glittered in the summer sunlight.

Here Kit Carson joined the party and was warmly
greeted by Frémont and his men—especially those who

had become acquainted with him and had come to rely on him the year before.

And so the expedition went forward, sometimes traveling no more than five or six miles a day, sometimes covering more than twenty. Occasionally Frémont split the party into two groups, each taking a different route, with instructions to meet at a spot farther on. Near Long's Peak, while Frémont was searching for a pass over the Rockies, an Indian woman with her two half-breed children came into camp and asked to be allowed to join the expedition on its march westward. She was a Shoshone, the widow of a Frenchman who had been murdered, and wanted to rejoin her own people who lived near Fort Bridger. The hospitable Frémont told her that she would be welcome, and from there on the two children added much to the liveliness of camp life, while the woman helped in many ways. She taught Frémont a great deal about edible roots, showing him which were wholesome, and where to dig for them. He paid special attention to the *Yampah*, or Indian potato, which was considered the best of all the roots for eating.

Two hundred miles from St. Vrain's Fort, camp was made in a narrow ravine near the north fork of the Platte. Buffalo were abundant there and some of the meat was cut into strips and hung on scaffolds over fires to dry in order to provide food in the mountains where Frémont knew that game would be scarce.

All hands were busy at this task when a man on guard saw an Indian looking over a hill at the camp. He gave the alarm, and the men of the camp had barely time to take defensive positions and wheel the howitzer into position well in the front when, with a high-pitched war cry, about seventy mounted Indians charged the camp. As they came closer, they all seemed to see the howitzer at the same time and to realize the strength of the Frémont party. So quickly did they pull their horses to a halt that it was as if the party, as one man, went from high speed into motionlessness without slowing down first. Then the leader made a sign of peace and the horses came on slowly.

Nevertheless the Frémont men maintained their vigilance as the Indians explained that they were a war party of Arapaho and Cheyenne Indians returning from an expedition against the Shoshones. They had mistaken the Frémont party, the leader said, for Shoshones, which was, Frémont wrote later,

. . . an excuse which policy required us to receive as true, though under the full conviction that . . . our little howitzer and our favorable position . . . certainly saved our horses, and probably ourselves, from their marauding intentions. . . . The pipe went round, provisions were spread, and the tobacco and goods furnished the customary presents. . . . After remaining until nearly sunset, they took their departure. . .

When they reached South Pass, Frémont found that there were now several roads through it, somewhat separated from one another. All had been made by emigrants seeking the easiest way over the mountains, and the number of trails showed clearly how greatly western emigration had increased in a year. They were now, Frémont calculated, about halfway between the Mississippi and the Pacific Ocean.

From the pass the expedition followed the Green River, or, as the Spaniards called it, the Rio Verde, a tributary of the Colorado, in what is now Utah. A mile or two away from Fort Bridger, the Shoshone woman and her two children quietly left the party.

Even when there were no emigrant trains in sight, the signs of their passing were frequent all along the trail. Here and there a solitary grave with a wooden marker mutely told a story of sorrow. Sometimes they passed a broken-down, abandoned wagon. On the western fork of the Laramie River Frémont had one day looked casually at a group of buffalo bulls, then had rubbed his eyes and looked again. All but one was the usual dun, grayish-brown. The exception was as red as Aunt Millie's red cow. As Frémont and the others rode closer, the grayish-brown animals lumbered away in an awkward but swift gallop, their heads down, their hoofs raising a cloud of dust. But the red one stood still, quite unafraid of the men approaching on horseback. When they got close to it, they saw that it was without doubt a domestic red ox.

Frémont wrote in his *Memoirs:*

We gathered around him as if he had been an old acquaintance. . . . He had probably made his escape from some party of emigrants on Green River; and with a vivid remembrance of some old green field, he was pursuing the straightest course for the frontier that the country admitted. We carried him along with us as a prize; and when it was found in the morning that he had wandered off, I would not let him be pursued, for I would rather have gone through a starving time of three entire days than let him be killed after he had successfully run the gauntlet so far among the Indians.

On another day a cow, followed by a calf, strayed into camp, and most amiably furnished milk for the evening coffee. Still later, at a time when the expedition was woefully short of meat, two stray, half-grown calves, wandering along the trail, furnished them with a meal of veal. On another day a half-starved dog with a bullet wound in his side wandered into camp and, attaching himself to the expedition, soon became a pet of all the men.

Wagon trains and camps were encountered much more often than they had been the year before. Frémont described one group of such camps:

The edge of the wood, for several miles along the river, was dotted with the white covers of emigrant wagons, collected . . . at different camps, where the smokes were rising lazily from the fires, around which the women were occupied in preparing the evening meal, and the children playing in the grass; and herds of cattle, grazing about in the bottom, had an air of quiet security and civilized comfort that made a rare sight for the traveller in such a remote wilderness.

The Oregon Trail was rapidly becoming a well-traveled highway.

At Great Salt Lake, Frémont, Preuss, Carson, Bernier, and Lajeunesse went in a rubber boat to an island on which Frémont believed no human being had previously set foot. Since they were short of salt they brought back with them five gallons of the water which, when boiled down, made seven quarts of fine white salt, according to Frémont's record. A week was spent in exploring the region, which Frémont considered suitable for a settlement or a military post. It was his report that induced Brigham Young to lead the Mormons there four years later to establish what is now Salt Lake City.

Traveling in the mountains, the supply of buffalo meat they had dried was soon exhausted, and it was necessary to send hunting parties far afield. Sometimes they were able to buy wild berries from the Indians. One day a freshly killed antelope was bought from an Indian for a little powder and shot. On September 14, while waiting hungrily for Fitzpatrick and a hunting party to return with meat, Frémont reluctantly gave the men permission to kill and eat a horse bought from the Snake Indians. But neither Frémont nor Preuss would eat any of the meat, "preferring," as Frémont wrote later, "to starve a little longer—feeling as much saddened as if a crime had been committed." From an encampment of Snake Indians they bought a small quantity of an edible root called *kooyah*. Later Frémont, giving an Indian boy a knife, induced the lad to identify the plant for him, and show him where it could be found, so that he and his men could dig it themselves.

On September 18 the expedition entered the plain of the Columbia River. Now they were in Oregon and nearing the end of their western march, and here eleven men left the expedition to return home before winter set in. But the rest of the group pushed on.

Following the Snake River, they came to a series of cataracts called Fishing Falls because it was so favorable a place for salmon fishing. Here they found a settlement of friendly Snake Indians who exchanged dried salmon for goods, and told Frémont that when the fish came upstream to spawn in the spring they were so thick that one could cast a spear in the river without looking and be sure to pierce a salmon. The Indians were very poor, but cheerful and seemingly happy. There was little game nearby that could furnish skins for clothing, and most of their garments were made of grass. So, instead of offering them beads, trinkets, or powder and shot in trade, Frémont showed them cloth and clothing. For these they traded eagerly.

Soon the expedition reached Fort Boise, a Hudson's Bay Company post, and a fortnight later approached the point at which the Snake, the Columbia, the Yakima, and the Walla Walla rivers join to form the lower Columbia. To the west they could see the snow-covered top of Mount Hood, one hundred and eighty miles away. Here they visited the famous mission of Dr. Marcus Whitman.

Frémont was deeply impressed by the majestic lower Columbia. "Here," he wrote, "we saw for the first time the great river on which the course of events for the last half century has been directing attention and conferring historical fame. The river is indeed a noble object and has here attained its full magnitude." The expedition was now about a thousand miles from South Pass and about two thousand from the junction of the Missouri and Kansas rivers.

At the Dalles, a narrow rapids-filled chasm through which the Columbia flows, most of the party stayed behind while Frémont and Preuss, with two other men, went on by canoe to Fort Vancouver, far down the Columbia, in order to relate Frémont's exploration with that of Captain Charles Wilkes of the U.S. Navy who had earlier explored this part of the Pacific Coast.

Reluctantly the explorer abandoned the idea of going on the short distance that would have taken him to the Pacific. After the effort he had made to get to this point he would have liked to experience the satisfaction of seeing the ocean. But the rainy season was close upon them. He had talked over with Senator Benton a plan to return by a dangerous but exciting route that had never been traveled before, so far as anyone knew, from north to south, and that certainly had never been accurately mapped. By taking this route he would be able to map much of the great basin between the Rockies and the Sierras, including a large part of the territory now comprising Utah, Nevada, and New Mexico. He knew well that the dangers of crossing the Sierras in winter were grave. How grave they were, however, he was yet to discover.

Across the Sierras in Winter

✠

HE SMALL PARTY fought its way back up the rapids of the Columbia to the main camp, staying one night opposite a strange hole in the mountain on the other side of the river. An Indian guide told Frémont that it was the place from which the high winds, so prevalent in this region, came. It was called the Devil's Hole, and for some time the Indians had been planning to send one of their slaves to explore it, but had not yet done so. Frémont was strongly tempted to save them the trouble by exploring it himself, but thinking again of the winter that was nearly upon them, and the difficult task ahead, he decided not to. That night the wind increased and, by the next morning, had become such a gale that the party stayed in camp all day, perhaps wondering if the Indian tale was true, after all.

Back at the main camp, with the expedition refitted, and the men all aware of the danger ahead, the party of twenty-five men, a hundred and five horses and mules, and some live California cattle for food, set out along the way that would eventually take them home—if they were able to survive the hazards of their journey. At first the route lay generally southward. The most dangerous part of it would be the crossing of the Sierras from east to west at a point at which no regularly used pass existed. Frémont then intended to continue southward between the Pacific Ocean and the Sierras; then to go eastward through a known pass, and northeastward to the Rockies, which he would cross to reach the Arkansas River. Down this he would go to Bent's Fort, and home. It seems so simple when expressed in words; it was, in fact, incredibly difficult.

A new member had been added to the expedition—a Chinook Indian. The young man had asked to be included in the party so that he could learn more about the ways of the white man.

The first objective was Lake Klamath (or, as Frémont called it, "Tlamath") in what is now southwest Oregon near the California border. To call it a lake was somewhat misleading. It consisted of an irregular depression about twenty miles in diameter which, for a short time in spring, was covered with water, but at other times of the year was simply a broad expanse of level grass dotted with shallow pools of water or spaces covered with ice, depending on the season.

As the expedition was about to start out, Frémont realized that the light wagon, that had safely carried all of the scientific instruments until now, was not fit for travel over the rugged mountain ways, so he left it behind to be given to Dr. Whitman's mission, and pushed on without it. The only thing on wheels now left in the party was the howitzer. But this soon became a burden, for, after the expedition had got into the mountains, the route often led down steep rocky precipices, which even the sure-footed mules descended with difficulty. At such places the howitzer had to be taken apart and let down by hand, piece by piece.

When they reached Lake Klamath, the temperature had dropped to zero, and all that reminded the men that they were facing a lake were patches of slick ice here and there, on which the animals found it difficult to keep their footing. As they rode on they saw ahead of them the smoke of a number of campfires. These, the guides told them, were the fires of a tribe of Klamath Indians, who were very warlike and untrustworthy. Hearing this, Frémont had the howitzer fire a shell that exploded a moment after the sound of the discharge. The double explosion was immediately effective. As if by magic, the smoke disappeared. So, too, did a few Indians who had approached to examine the party.

The next day Frémont, with a small party, sought and found the Indian village. As they came near it a band of natives rode out to meet them. To his surprise Frémont saw that a woman was among them. Never before had he seen a woman in an Indian war party. It was not until later, after he had convinced the Indians that he had come in peace and friendliness, that he found the explanation. The woman was the wife of the chief. When the tribe had heard the double explosion the day before, all had become convinced that they were about to be slaughtered, and that there was nothing they could do to prevent it. As head man the chief had decided that it was his duty to face the danger first, and, learning that he was riding to meet it, his wife had insisted upon going along to be killed with him!

Frémont saw at a glance that the Indians were very poor. The village consisted of a group of circular huts about twenty feet in diameter. The only entrance to each hut was a door in the roof. There was little game in the region, but the Indians had made the most of the fact that they were surrounded by an abundance of coarse, strong grass, and had used it in every possible way—for shoes, baskets, basket-like caps for the women, colored mats about four feet square, and other things. A number of wolf-like dogs sat on the tops of the houses. Frémont took a fancy to a frisky and affectionate young one, bought it, and named it Klamath. He also bought a number of the grass mats for his men to lay between their blankets and the snow.

He tried to obtain guides for the next stage of his journey, but all the Indians refused to go, regardless of the rewards he offered. They knew what a winter in the Sierras was like. Some men would perhaps have taken warning from this and abandoned the hazardous trip, but Frémont and his men pushed on.

The following day the chief of the Klamath Indians caught up with them, accompanied by two of his tribesmen. He said that he was ashamed of his lack of hospitality in letting them leave without guides and that he had brought these two men to show the way. But they did not stay with the party long. On December 14 the expedition fought its way for seven hours through a

heavy snowstorm in a pine forest. The guides, who were
scantily clad, refused to go farther. By signs, and by
maps drawn in the snow, they indicated that the expedition was now approaching a point at which several small
rivers joined to make a large one. The explorer thought,
wrongly, that this must be the Sacramento, which emptied into San Francisco Bay. Then the Indians, thanking
Frémont for the generous presents that he gave them,
turned and started back to Lake Klamath and their snug
round houses with the tight doors on the roofs.

Two days later the expedition was still climbing
through a pine forest of magnificently tall and large
trees. The snow was about three feet deep and seemed
to grow deeper with every step forward. It was heavily
crusted, and cut the animals' feet and ankles as they
broke through. Frémont wrote:

The air was dark with falling snow, which everywhere
weighed down the trees. The depths of the forest were pro-
foundly still. . . . I found that it required some exertion of
constancy to adhere steadily to one course through the
woods, when we were uncertain how far the forest extended,
or what lay beyond; and on account of our animals it would
be bad to spend another night in the mountain.

Suddenly they rode into a rocky spot without trees
and found themselves at the top of a vertical, rocky wall.
More than a thousand feet below them lay a sunlit green
prairie in which there was a beautiful lake some twenty
miles long. It was an incredible contrast to the snow-

storm all about them. But seeing the delightful spot below them and reaching it were two different things. They rode four or five miles to the north, making several unsuccessful attempts to descend. Finally the descent was made, with great difficulty but without casualties, though one of the mules lost its footing and, with its pack, rolled over and over down a steep slope.

They were able to enjoy the pleasant surroundings only briefly. Soon they were climbing again, once more through snow-covered forests. Often they encountered small groups of strange Indians of unknown tribes.

Christmas day found them at Lake Warner in southern Oregon. Here they celebrated by firing the howitzer and small arms and drinking toasts in brandy. On December 28 they came upon two isolated huts which had been suddenly abandoned. The huts were open at the top, a sage fire was burning in the middle of each one, straw baskets and rabbit skins were lying about, and piles of grass showed where the inhabitants had been sleeping. A number of Indians were scrambling up the side of a hill shouting "Tabibo-bo," which Frémont later learned meant "white." As Carson approached them they ran off like deer. A woman with two children had dropped behind a sage bush and when Carson, not seeing them there, stumbled against her, she shut her eyes in terror and began to scream, obviously thinking she was about to be killed.

Gradually, with presents, signs, and a kindly tone of voice in which he spoke words the Indians did not understand, Frémont quieted them and learned of their extreme poverty and primitive ways. They were of the Snake tribe, living eight or ten in one small shelter, eating edible roots and rabbits killed in the sage brush. Their scanty clothing was made of rabbit skins. Apparently they had never before seen white men.

Here the grazing was so sparse that all of the animals were suffering from lack of food and becoming weaker. On January 3, every man in the expedition dismounted. The loads of the pack animals were redistributed and shared by the animals the men had been riding, so that each carried less. That day the expedition camped by the dry bed of a stream, where there was grass but no water. Several horses and two mules had already collapsed from weakness. By the sixth, fifteen animals had been lost. It was not until nine days later that they reached a spot by a fine fresh water stream where there was grass for the animals, and salmon trout brought by friendly Indians from a nearby village. Men and animals rested here and regained some of their strength.

On January 15, the expedition camped near the place that is now Reno, Nevada. Here Frémont announced to the men his determination to cross the Sierras into California, then the property of Mexico. The Mexican government had forbidden Americans to enter the territory, and the hazards of crossing the Sierras in winter were so great as to make the venture seem foolhardy. The massive range rises precipitously from east to west, in some places 14,500 feet high. There are few passes, and in 1844 those that existed were largely unknown. There were no maps available. The summits of the peaks were silent expanses of deep snow, on which trails, poorly marked at best, were completely hidden. Sub-zero temperatures and driving blizzards were commonplace.

Yet without hesitation, and without giving men and animals enough rest, Frémont set out on January 19, in the worst month of the year! He knew that the British coveted the rich territory, and that any knowledge he could acquire about the region would help the United States eventually to annex it.

As the party climbed, it became more and more difficult to transport the howitzer. Often a great deal of time was lost getting it up or down steep slopes. Finally, on January 29, Frémont decided that it was not worth the effort necessary to keep it with the expedition and reluctantly abandoned it. It had accompanied them all the way from St. Louis, had twice frightened the Indians and kept them from making an attack, and had boomed out cheerily on Christmas morning. But there was little choice. One wonders what the Indians of the region thought of it when they found it lying on a mountain slope with no one near it!

That evening, as the party was settling down for the night, a number of almost naked Indians came quietly into the camp, showing neither fear nor hostility, and settled down around the fires, curiously watching every move of the white men. They were armed with bows and arrows and some carried large nets, thirty or forty feet long, made of wild hemp. With these they had been trapping rabbits. No one in the Frémont party could understand their language, but by clear signs they warned Frémont against trying to cross the mountains in winter, indicating that the snow (which they called *táh-ve*) was higher than a man's head, that anyone trying to cross it would quickly perish, and that it would be wise for them to go back down the mountain. They even offered to conduct them to a lake filled with fish.

Among them was a young man whom Frémont described as very intelligent, who was induced to act as a guide. Everyone in the party liked him and named him "Mélo," which, in the language of his tribe meant "friend." He had seen white men before, he said, and he swore, first by the sky, and then by the earth, that what he said was true.

As the party climbed, the snow became deeper and deeper. Soon it became necessary to break a road. This was done by ten men, each on a strong horse. One would go ahead, sometimes on foot, leading his horse, and sometimes on horseback, trampling down the snow until he and his mount were exhausted; then he would step aside and fall to the rear while the next in line would take the lead.

Five days later, attempting to ascend a slope the guide had pointed out, the best horses gave out and refused to make an effort to climb. The guide, as well as the men of the expedition, thought it was useless to try to go on, but Frémont refused to give the order to go back. The animals were unloaded, the equipment and supplies were left lying along the newly broken trail, and the horses, under a strong guard, were left on a flat open space where the snow had blown away enough to expose a few patches of grass. That night the men had no shelter. Around the trunk of a large pine they spread small pine boughs. Over these they put the grass mats that Frémont had bought from the Klamath Indians, and their blankets, and got what rest they could in a temperature of 10° above zero with a high wind.

An old Indian visited the expedition at this camp and with signs and loud words warned them all of the futility of trying to go any farther. Frémont had by now learned some of the Indian speech of the region, and was able to make out the somber words, repeated over and over, "rock upon rock—rock upon rock—snow upon snow—snow upon snow!" Frémont wrote:

He made us the signs of precipices, and showed us how the horses' feet would slip and throw them off the narrow trails which led along their sides. Our Chinook, who comprehended even more readily than ourselves, and believed our situation hopeless, covered his head with his blanket and began to weep and lament. "I wanted to see the whites," said he; "I came away from my own people to see the whites, and I wouldn't care to die among them . . ."

That night it was too cold to sleep and everyone was miserable. In the morning Mélo, obviously badly frightened, was shivering by the fire, and Frémont, moved by the lad's misery, threw one of his own blankets around him. A few minutes later both Mélo and the blanket were missing and no one in the expedition ever saw either again. The rest of the day was spent making sledges and snowshoes.

From this point a track had to be made by an advance party tramping down the snow with snowshoes. Then loaded sledges were drawn along the trail by hand, after which it was left to freeze overnight. In the morning it was hard enough to bear the weight of the animals. Thus men, sledges, and animals were able, with care, to cross snow that ranged in depth from five to twenty feet, as Frémont was able to determine by the height of the snow against the tree trunks.

For a month the party fought its way through all of the hardships the aged Indian had foretold—"rock upon rock—snow upon snow—." Food became scarce. Sometimes they had to kill a horse or mule in order to avoid starvation. Other animals collapsed and died of exhaustion and starvation. Even the Indian dog Klamath, fat now, reluctantly was put into the pot. Here and there they were able to buy pinyon nuts (the seeds of the nut pine) and edible acorns from the Indians.

Many of the men were almost blinded by the glare of the snow, but they tied handkerchiefs over their eyes and stumbled on.

On February 9 and 10, Frémont, leading an advance party to beat down the trail, was able to proceed only five and a half miles. But Frémont would not give up. He had the men make mauls, and with these and shovels they cleared away the deep snow in places and beat it down in others, strengthening it with pine boughs.

The animals had been left behind at camp under heavy guard, in charge of Fitzpatrick. When Fitzpatrick tried to bring the rest of the party forward, the animals

*Captain John
Augustus Sutter*

floundered and broke through the snow. Some sank and
were buried in it. The others refused to go on. By March
6 only 33 horses and mules were left of the 105 with
which the party had set out from the Columbia, and the
courage of the men had reached a low ebb. But on that
day they entered a pleasantly clean, neat, large Indian
village. Here they met a well-dressed Indian who, in
excellent Spanish, told them he was a cowhand working
for Captain Sutter, and offered to escort them to Sutter's
ranch and fort. (Sutter had already become a legend in
the West. In 1839 he had obtained a grant of over 57,000

acres of land from the Mexican government—land on which the city of Sacramento now stands. Here he had established what amounted to a small, self-sufficient private kingdom, capable of supplying all his needs.)

The spirits of the men rose as they followed the Indian to the collection of adobe buildings that constituted Sutter's Fort. The party was admitted by an Indian guard, and Frémont was amazed by what he found within the walls. There were quarters for troops, workshops, a blacksmith, a distillery, a residence, and other buildings. Many men were employed by the captain—Indians, Mexicans, Hawaiians, and white Americans who had stopped in on their way westward and stayed. A woolen factory was being constructed, and Sutter said he had a number of Indian girls in training who would work it.

The flour mill was very like the mills used by primitive man. Two millstones, quarried in the Sierras, one sitting upon the other, provided the chief mechanism. Mules were hitched to a long sweep attached to the top stone, and walked slowly round and round. The flour, middlings, and bran, were then separated from one another by sieves.

The distillery made a sort of brandy out of wine pressed from wild grapes that grew abundantly in the Sacramento valley.

A bountiful welcome feast was served to the explorer and his men. They who had known near starvation now sat down to trout and salmon, fresh from the water, roast venison, bear meat, smoked tongue, ham and fine steaks,

Sutter's Fort

peas, salad, and fruits, with good Rhine wine to mark the meal as a festive occasion.

During the days that followed, Frémont saw all that he could of Sutter's vast domain, and talked to as many of the men as possible while the workmen were busy shoeing his animals, outfitting them with saddles and bridles, and selecting fresh horses and cattle. Many of the men, Frémont learned, were not happy about the conditions under which they lived and would rather be protected by the strong government of the United States than to be under Mexican rule. This was the kind of knowledge Frémont stored in his mind for future use.

It was a strange procession that moved out of Sutter's Fort on March 24 to start southward. In the van and on the flanks rode the scouts. A detachment rode behind the forward scouts, and another brought up the rear. Between these two groups were the pack animals, the baggage, and the provisions. The animals, replenished at Sutter's Fort, now consisted of 130 horses and mules, and about 30 cattle, including some milch cows. The course now lay for 500 miles southward between the Sierras and the Pacific Ocean to a pass at the head of the San Joaquin River. Going east through the pass the expedition would travel southeast to the Spanish Trail which connected the small settlement called Pueblo di Nuestra Senora de Los Angeles (which has grown into the great sprawling city of Los Angeles) with Santa Fe. At the Colorado the course would turn northeast and take the expedition back to Great Salt Lake, and from there to the Rockies, and thence home.

It was while the expedition was on the first leg of this course that Frémont was able to explode a myth and correct a widely spread mistaken idea of the geography of the West. One of the objectives of the hazardous trip across the Sierras was to locate, if possible, the much talked of Rio Buenaventura, believed to be a great stream connecting the interior of the United States with the Pacific Ocean. Frémont's report of the facts was short and positive:

No river from the interior does, or can, cross the Sierra Nevada—itself more lofty than the Rocky Mountains. The Buenaventura . . . is, in fact, a small stream of no consequence . . . falling into the Pacific near Monterey. There is no opening from the Bay of San Francisco into the interior of the continent.

The trip southward and through the easy pass east of the Pueblo de Los Angeles was comparatively uneventful. But once on the Spanish Trail a real adventure overtook them. On April 24, two Mexicans—a man named Andres Fuentes, and a boy of eleven named Pablo Hernandez—burst into camp, wild-eyed, and frantic, with a pitiful story. They belonged, they said, to a party of traders from New Mexico. Six of the party, including Fuentes and Pablo, Fuentes' wife, Pablo's mother and father, and another man, had been left to guard the horses while the rest of the party left to trade. Attacked by a band of about thirty Indians, Fuentes and Pablo had charged through the Indian lines on their horses, and thus had become separated from the other four. The Indians had driven off all of their horses save the two that the man and boy rode. Fuentes was afraid that his wife had been carried away as a captive, and Pablo already thought of himself as an orphan.

Frémont and Carson promised the two whatever help they could give. Carson and Alexander Godey volunteered to ride after the marauders, to bring horses and captives back if possible, and if not, to avenge their death. They started at once, taking Fuentes with them. The Mexican's horse soon gave out and he had to return, but Carson and Godey went on.

The following night was dark, but the two men, Godey only a little less skilled in mountain lore than Carson himself, kept traveling, walking, and leading their horses, often following the trail by feeling. Just as the sun was rising the next morning they saw the Indians, encamped about two miles farther on and enjoying a breakfast of horse steaks. Now began the difficult part of their mission. They were two against thirty. The only attack that could possibly succeed was one of complete surprise. They left their horses hidden in a clump of trees and crawled on their bellies toward the camp, hoping to come unseen into the herd of stolen horses.

All went well until they were actually among the animals. Then a young horse, frightened by the crawling figures of two men, began to snort and kick up its heels. This alarmed the rest of the herd, who stirred restlessly, making the Indians reach for their weapons.

Now Kit and Godey, with a shrill war yell, charged

the camp. When they were within rifle range they stopped, each picked out an Indian, and fired. Kit brought his man down with a fatal wound; Godey had to reload and fire again before another fell. Thoroughly cowed now, and doubtless thinking that these two mad-men were the advance guard of a large body of armed white men, the Indians scattered. The two white men now rounded up the stolen horses and found that all but five of them were there. The five missing had doubtless been butchered by the Indians for food.

At the site of the camp from which the Mexicans had been driven, they found the bodies of the two men who had been left on guard, pierced with arrows, and man-gled by tomahawks. There was no trace of the two women.

May was also marked by tragedy. On May 8 Kit Carson reported that one of the expedition's best men, Tabeau, who had back-tracked to search for a lame mule that was missing, had not returned and was overdue. Even while Carson and Frémont were talking about it they saw smoke rise suddenly from a group of cotton-woods nearby. Kit immediately interpreted it as an In-dian signal telling others that a blow had been struck against the white men, and warning other Indians to be on their guard against reprisals.

A detachment was immediately sent out, in charge of Carson, to look for the missing man, but he was never found. The mortally wounded mule was, however. And not far from the dying animal there was an area where blood on the leaves and beaten-down grass showed where Tabeau had fought a valiant but obviously losing battle for his life. From the spot where the fight had taken place, there was a trail of blood leading to a nearby river into which the body, stripped of clothing and all possessions, had apparently been thrown. The horse he had been riding was nowhere in evidence, having almost certainly been driven off by the Indians.

Two weeks later another of the men, François Badeau, was killed when he drew a gun toward him by the muzzle. The hammer of the weapon, striking against some obstacle on the ground, was accidentally discharged, driving the ball through his head.

On May 23 Frémont and his party reached Utah Lake, near Great Salt Lake, and on the last day of July encamped once more at Kansas Landing, from which, over a year before, they had hurried on receipt of Jessie's letter. Now the wilderness was behind them. From here it was a comparatively simple trip down the river to St. Louis, where the party was disbanded, a number of them to meet again the following year in the third expedition to the West.

As Frémont and his men had said good-by, each of them looked forward to the possibility of meeting again, if and when Frémont led another expedition. Kit Carson's plans were uncertain. He had been a wanderer for a long time. Now, perhaps, he would settle down. But, taking his leader's hand in a strong grip, the seasoned mountaineer had promised that, whatever he did, if Frémont ever needed him, he had only to send word and, regardless of where he was or what he was doing, Carson would come. Frémont treasured this promise, and stored it away in his mind for possible future use.

The Pathfinder was to make more hazardous mountain trips, but he was never to forget his first crossing of the Sierra. Nor were others. Ten years later, when Frémont was a candidate for the presidency of the United States, John Greenleaf Whittier, his friend and supporter, commemorated the crossing in the following poem:

THE PASS OF THE SIERRA

All night above their rocky bed
They saw the stars march slow;
The wild Sierra overhead,
The desert's death below.

The Indian from his lodge of bark,
The gray bear from his den,
Beyond their camp-fire's wall of dark,
Glared on the mountain men.

Still upward turned, with anxious strain,
Their leader's sleepless eye,
Where splinters of the mountain chain
Stood black against the sky.

Rise up Frémont! and go before
The Hour must have its Man;
Put on thy hunting shirt once more,
And lead in Freedom's van!

Hero's Homecoming

☩

WHEN FRÉMONT reached St. Louis in August 1844, he was amazed at how much it had grown since he had left it fourteen months earlier. Now it was a city of 30,000 and a great river port. The wharfs were crowded with migrants, traders, trappers, and ranchers on their way westward. This was the doorway to the West. This was still the last civilized point of call for many many miles on the way to the Pacific.

It was after midnight when Frémont's boat docked, and he dashed down the gangplank, to be one of the first on shore. At that late hour there were no hacks, so he started off at a brisk walk, which sometimes became a run, toward the Benton house where he expected to find Jessie waiting for him. When he got there he threw pebbles at a window of old Gabriel's room over the carriage house to waken him. The Benton coachman came to the window, rubbing his eyes sleepily.

"Marss Frémont," he called, "is dat really *you*, or is it a ghost?"

Frémont smiled and asked, "Can you let me into the house quietly? Is Mrs. Frémont well?"

"Yes sir, she is, and I can let you in," Gabriel answered, "but she's at Miss Anne's taking care of Mrs. Potts, who's sick."

With that Frémont turned and ran off into the dark so quickly that later Gabriel reported that he without doubt had seen Marss Frémont's ghost!

Miss Anne was a cousin of Jessie's, and wife of the Reverend Mr. Potts, of the Presbyterian Church. Frémont rushed to the parsonage, expecting to wake the family and go at once to Jessie, but as he came near to the house he remembered that Mrs. Potts was ill, and feared that an alarm in the night might bring on a relapse, so he took up a watching position on a bench in front of the Barnum Hotel across the street. Already a dim light in the east announced the approach of dawn, and in a few moments the door of the hotel was opened by an employee, who, recognizing Frémont, came out and offered him a room in which to get a little sleep before the day began. On the first real bed he had known in over fourteen months, he slept for several hours.

Meanwhile Gabriel had risen early and hurried to the house to tell the Benton family about the strange apparition he had seen and the ghostly voice he had heard after midnight. Since Frémont was now nowhere in evidence, and since rumors had long been current in St. Louis that he had been lost in the Sierras, it now seemed obvious to the good old man that he had indeed been talking with a ghost. The Bentons at once sent a message to the parsonage, where Jessie was wakened and told. But no one there had seen the returned traveler, and

Gabriel's ghost theory was accepted—at least by the servants. The baby's nurse set up a weeping and keening that continued until Frémont walked in.

His reunion with Jessie was a joyous one. But they had no chance for a real talk alone until late that evening, for the news of the hero's return spread like a prairie fire, and all day long friends swarmed into the house to welcome him. It was late that night before he was able to learn of the ordeal through which Jessie had gone during his absence.

She had received no word from or of him since he had left the lower Columbia in November 1843. At the coming of the new year she had made herself believe that he would arrive any day, so each night she set a place for him at the supper table and left a light burning near a window. As spring drew near, a rumor reached Jessie's friends, brought from trappers and traders who had come from the west to St. Louis to get supplies, that Frémont had gone into the Sierras after deep winter had set in, and had disappeared. The rumor was not repeated to Jessie, but the solicitude of her friends, their obvious concern, and their added tenderness to her, made her suspicious that they knew something that she did not, and her anxiety increased. But still she kept her high faith that he was alive and would return soon. Secretary of War William Wilkins offered to send a company of dragoons into the Sierras to search for him, but Jessie and others who knew him best pointed out that if he was where the dragoons could find him he would himself be able to find his way out of the mountains.

Now her faith was justified and, for a little time, at least, she and her husband and their young daughter, Lilly, could lead a normal family life together.

There were a few responsibilities to be discharged before Frémont went to Washington. He had brought Pablo with him—the Mexican orphan whose mother had been kidnapped and whose father had been killed by the Indians; also two California Indian boys, Juan and Gregorio; the Chinook Indian boy who was actually a young man now, by Indian standards, being eighteen; and his own fine saddle horse, Sacramento, which he had bought in California. As quickly as possible he made arrangements for their welfare until they could rejoin him. Pablo was left with the Bentons in St. Louis. Juan, Gregorio, and Sacramento went to the family's Kentucky farm.

With these matters arranged, Jessie, Frémont, and their daughter went to Washington. Chinook went along and, as a temporary ward of the Indian Bureau, he went later to live with a Quaker family in Philadelphia in order to get a little of the white man's education. Frémont's return was saddened by the fact that no welcome waited for him from two old friends, Nicollet and Hassler. Both had died during his absence, Nicollet alone in a hotel room. "It would have been a fitter end for him," Frémont wrote later, "to have died under the open sky, and been buried rolled up in a blanket by the side of some stream in the mountains." He understood well the Frenchman's love of nature, for it had been in Nicollet's company that Frémont himself had learned to love the life out-of-doors.

In Washington the Frémonts lived with Senator Benton, but the explorer rented a small house nearby that he used as a workshop. Here he and Jessie worked together on his report, while an assistant, Joseph Hubbard, helped him with the map-making. Frémont would dictate to Jessie until one o'clock in the afternoon. At this time a servant would come in with the baby and a cold lunch. After eating the Frémonts would usually take the baby for a walk along the Potomac.

For several nights Frémont and Hubbard went out late to test a sextant near a church where there were few passersby, and where there was a large stone carriage step. While waiting for the stars he wished to observe, Frémont sprawled easily, half lying, against the carriage step, sometimes as late as one or two o'clock in the morning.

One afternoon as Jessie and her husband entered the Benton house after their walk, they heard Senator Benton speaking angrily in the library. The senator heard their footsteps and called them in. With him was a deacon who lived across from the church. As Frémont and Jessie walked in, the senator said angrily to his caller, "I want you to repeat to Mr. and Mrs. Frémont what you have just told me!"

The deacon, his face red, tried to evade the demand, but the senator insisted, and finally the churchman blurted out that on several occasions he had seen Frémont and a companion very late at night so drunk that they had not been able to get home, and, as a consequence, were prostrate in front of the church. Frémont and Jessie both roared with laughter, and, after the senator had pointed out to the deacon the danger of placing the worst possible interpretation on an event without knowing the truth, the man departed, silent with embarrassment.

The report of Frémont's second expedition was finished on March 1, 1845, and printed by order of Congress. The printing order this time included an extra 10,000 copies, and also 10,000 more copies of the report of the first expedition.

While Frémont had been working on the report, Washington had been buzzing with talk about the possibility of war with Mexico. Texas had been an independent republic since its war with Mexico had culminated in the victory of Sam Houston at San Jacinto in 1836. Mexico, none too happy about having lost this great expanse of land, was now deeply disturbed by the possibility that Texas might be annexed to the United States. Among the usually well informed there was speculation that the United States must choose between leaving Texas as it was, or annexing it at the cost of war with its neighbor to the south.

Early in March 1845 the Congress adopted a resolution annexing Texas, which was greeted in Mexico by a burst of anger and demands for a declaration of war. The Mexican government immediately broke off diplomatic relations with the United States. The Mexican Army was mobilized and munitions rushed to Matamoras on the northern border. Yet not a gun was fired,

*President
James Knox Polk*

and the United States government, still hoping to avoid open hostilities, waited for Mexico to move.

Other possible causes of armed conflict lay in the Far West from which the explorer had just returned. Polk was inaugurated as President of the United States, succeeding Tyler, Congress opened, and the expansionist policy of the new government soon became evident. This meant not only the probable annexation of Texas, but also a vigorous attempt to acquire California, by peaceful agreement if possible, by force if necessary, and to settle once and for all the controversy between the United States and Great Britain over the control of Oregon—to settle it, that is, by making it clear that the United States would be in sole control. It was a delicate situation in which both Mexico and Great Britain were involved. Britain's interest in the West Coast, and her desire to hold on to whatever claim she might have, or feel that she had, to Oregon, could well result in her moving into California if the United States went to war with Mexico.

Frémont knew that in some ways his report added fuel to the fire. For, among other things, he was making California and Oregon more attractive by pointing out the errors in various reports about the West. For instance, a book that had just been published in England by an employee of the Hudson's Bay Company contained such absurd statements as this:

Though several parties have penetrated into the Oregon Territory from the United States through the gorges of the Rocky Mountains . . . the difficulties are so numerous and formidable . . . that there is no secure, expeditious, or commodious track which can ever be used as a highway.

An American traveler named Townsend wrote in a similar vein. Frémont corrected this impression in his report. Already the Oregon Trail had become a well-traveled highway. Today railroads and concrete automobile highways follow the trails that Frémont and his contemporaries blazed.

After the inauguration Frémont made a courtesy call on President Polk. In the course of their talk Frémont mentioned a map of the West in the Congressional Library which showed that the Great Salt Lake of Utah was connected with the Pacific Ocean by three large rivers, and reported that his own observations had disproved this, adding that the Sierras made it impossible. The President smiled and said something about "the impulsiveness of youth," adding that he had great respect for these old maps, and that he was not at all sure that the three rivers which the map showed did not indeed flow from the Great Salt Lake to the Pacific Ocean! The explorer was speechless, but decided not to argue the matter with the President.

Despite President Polk's opinion of the young man's "impulsiveness," he approved of a signal honor awarded the explorer—a double brevet, a rarely used promotion, that made him a first lieutenant and a captain at one stroke, thus avoiding the waiting time that usually ensues between two promotions.

During the spring, plans for the third expedition were perfected. It was made known that Frémont's purpose would be to explore the part of the Rockies in which the Arkansas rises, the Rio Grande del Norte (today known simply as the Rio Grande) which empties into the Gulf of Mexico, and the Colorado River, which empties into the Gulf of California. A more detailed examination of the Salt Lake region was also to be made, and further explorations to take place in the Cascade and Sierra Nevada ranges—a large order indeed. But Frémont recorded in his *Memoirs* that he was given orders that were not made public and which were to be followed in case of war with Mexico. What these orders were was never made clear, but his later conduct may be a clue to them, when his role as an explorer and mapmaker was abandoned for a more belligerent one.

The young Chinook was called back from Philadelphia. He arrived carrying a large family Bible. Opening it proudly to the place provided for the Family Record he laughed and said, "Chinook put here name all wife and all horse!"

Many men from the second expedition rejoined Frémont at St. Louis, including Godey and Basil Lajeunesse. Twelve Delaware Indians also joined the white men. Among them were two chiefs named Swanok and Sagundai. Juan, Gregorio, and Frémont's fine saddle

One of the Delaware bodyguard

horse Sacramento were recalled from the farm, other men were added, equipment was assembled, and on August 2, 1845, Frémont arrived at Bent's Fort with sixty well-armed, well-mounted, and well-equipped men. He knew, as few others did, that this expedition might, overnight, change from an exploratory to a military operation. But how important a part he was about to play in making California one of the United States of America not even he knew.

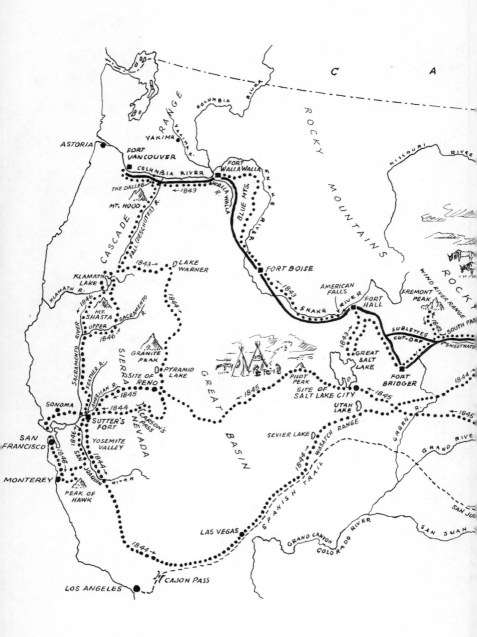

116

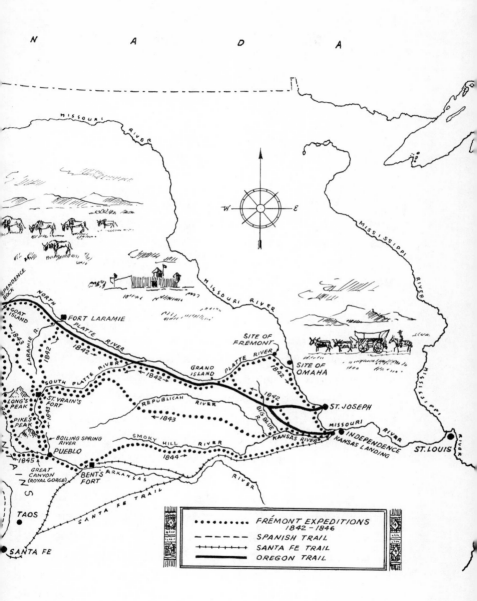

FRÉMONT EXPEDITIONS
1842 – 1846
SPANISH TRAIL
SANTA FE TRAIL
OREGON TRAIL

The Road to War

✠

URING THE SPRING of 1845, while Frémont was in Washington reporting on his second expedition, and mapping much of the territory he had visited, Kit Carson was busy with a new project that seemed to preclude the possibility of his joining Frémont on another expedition. Kit the hunter, Kit the wanderer, Kit the Indian fighter, Kit the favorite exploring partner of Frémont, had decided to settle down to one of the world's oldest and most peaceable occupations. He was in the process of becoming a farmer!

After years of loneliness following the death of his first wife, he had married again and was making a home for his wife and himself. With Richard Owens, an old friend and mountaineering companion, he had bought a tract of wild land forty-five miles east of Taos, New Mexico. Here, on the banks of the Cimarron River, they had settled, with farm implements, stock, and Mexican laborers to help them build several adobe houses and work the land, and had begun to till the soil. Grain was sowed, timber was cut to be used in building more substantial houses than the hastily thrown up huts of sun-baked clay, and Kit was looking forward with a quiet satisfaction to the time when he could harvest his first crop.

Into his happy speculation broke a horseman, riding at full speed, and bearing a letter from Frémont. Kit opened it thoughtfully and, with a grave face, read the words of his friend and former leader. Exactly what Frémont wrote is not recorded. It is obvious, however, that he reminded Kit of his promise to join him at any time and place he appointed, and that such a time and place were mentioned in the letter. Whether he wrote of the possibility of something beyond a third expedition of exploration or not is unknown, but it is certain that the possibility of war with Mexico was in Kit's mind as well as in Frémont's. The speed with which Kit arranged his affairs in order to keep his promise indicates that he may well have considered this a possible call to arms as well as to less violent adventure.

Frémont was, indeed, asking a great deal of his friend—more perhaps than he would have asked had he not realized that something beyond exploration would almost certainly concern the party of this third expedition. Carson had a large investment in his land, his stock, and his equipment; his marriage was to have been the beginning of a life of peace and quiet after long restlessness, and he must have gazed with some sadness at the pile of material that lay ready for the building of a substantial house for his wife and himself. Yet in four days he had sold all of his holding on the Cimarron, including land, stock, and equipment, for something like half of what it had cost him, had arranged with Governor Bent

Bent's Fort

to take care of his wife, and, with Dick Owens, was on his way to join his friend and leader.

On August 16 the explorer and his party of sixty, including Carson and Owens, left Bent's Fort and started westward. Among them was Lieutenant Abert of the Topographical Corps, a relative of its head, and James McDowell, Jessie's nephew. Preuss was not one of them, having been persuaded by his wife to buy a house in

Washington and stay there. He had been replaced by Edward M. Kern of Philadelphia, a young artist whose skill in sketching from nature—especially birds and plants—had a strong appeal to the nature-loving Frémont. Accompanying the men were two hundred horses and a few cattle, which would be used for food when game became scarce.

Much of the route that the expedition took now had been traveled by Frémont before, and the journey was comparatively uneventful. Two encounters with Indian women, however, are worth recording, not only as good stories but also because one of them demonstrates clearly Frémont's kindness, and the other his natural childlike playfulness and good will.

The expedition was encamped by a fine spring near the Great Basin. As they had approached it Chief Sagundai had pointed out tracks made by a woman's bare feet, but this was not an unusual occurrence in Indian country and no one paid much attention to them. Later they sat around the campfire in the little circle of light that made the darkness beyond seem even darker, eating a meal of freshly killed antelope. Kit Carson, who had been lying on the ground leaning on one elbow, sat up suddenly, and pointing across the fire, cried, "Good God! Look there!"

Frémont wrote later:

In the blaze of the fire, peering over her skinny, crooked hands . . . was standing an old woman apparently eighty years of age, nearly naked, her grizzly hair hanging down

"In the blaze of the fire, was standing an old woman"

over her face and shoulders. She had thought it a camp of
her people and had already begun to talk and gesticulate,
when her open mouth was paralyzed with fright, as she
saw the faces of the whites. She turned to escape, but the
men had gathered about her and brought her around to the
fire. Hunger and cold soon dispelled fear and she made us
understand that she had been left by her people at the
spring to die, because she was very old and could gather no
more seeds and was no longer good for anything. She told
us she had nothing to eat and was very hungry. We
gave her immediately about a quarter of the antelope, thinking she would roast it by our fire, but no sooner did she get
it in her hand than she darted off into the darkness. Someone ran after her with a brand of fire, but calling after her
brought no answer. In the morning, her fresh tracks at the
spring showed that she had been there for water during the
night. . . . Before we started we left for her at the spring a
little supply from what food we had. This, with what she
could gather from the nut-pine trees on the mountain, together with our fire, which she could easily keep up, would
probably prolong her life even after the snows came. The
nut-pines and cedars extend their branches out to the ground
and in one of their thickets, as I have often proved, these
make a comfortable shelter against the most violent snow-
storms.

Frémont knew the natives of this part of the West
well from earlier contacts.

In this region the condition of the Indian is nearly akin to
that of the lower animals. . . . The labor of their lives was to

get something to eat. The occupation of the women was in gleaning from the earth everything of vegetable or insect life; the occupation of the men was to kill every animal they could for food and every man of every other tribe for pleasure.

To Frémont there was something infinitely pathetic about the Indian, and in an old abandoned woman such as the one they found at Sagundai's spring, he saw the symbol of a vanishing race, being pushed aside by an advancing civilization and helpless to change its destiny. A kind man by nature, this understanding of the plight of the American aborigine increased his desire to help whenever possible. He restrained his Delawares from robbing or killing western Indians they encountered many times on this expedition. Because of this attitude, he was seldom treated as anything but a friend wherever he went, except by the most warlike tribes.

Some months after the depressing meeting with the old woman at Sagundai's spring, another, and much gayer, meeting occurred. Frémont and Godey were riding quietly along in a grove of oak trees when, at the top of a hill ahead of them, they saw two Indian women gathering plants and putting them in grass baskets. Apparently the women had not seen the two white men approaching, so in a spirit of pure fun Frémont decided to try to come up behind them and surprise them, as a child might approach a friend secretly, put his hands over the other's eyes, and say, "Guess who!" The two

Sagundai

men advanced stealthily, using the trees as cover. Sometimes they could see the women, sometimes they could not. When they reached the top of the hill and emerged from the trees for their surprise appearance, there were no women in sight. The baskets lay on the ground, their contents spilled. Nearby there were some low-growing bushes. Looking at them, Frémont suddenly burst into loud laughter and pointed. Godey saw two pairs of bare feet sticking out, which began to wiggle, as their owners rolled out of the bushes and joined in the laughter of the two white men. Then they hurried on to their village, apparently to spread the exciting news that there were friendly white men in the neighborhood, for later when the Frémont party reached a river near the village, the tribesmen helped them to cross it in canoes and small rafts. As he passed the village, Frémont noted with interest the beehive-shaped huts on the tops of which naked Indians happily sunned themselves, and a number of wicker cribs partly filled with acorns, which, like squirrels, the Indians had gathered and stored for winter food.

On December 9 the party reached Sutter's Fort and left five days later after having replenished their supplies and bought some fresh horses. They soon reached a place where the many bones of horses indicated that a band of savages, called "Horse Thief Indians" because they depended chiefly on stolen horses for their food, was nearby. Knowing how dangerous this tribe was, Frémont sent Dick Owens, Maxwell, and two Delaware Indians ahead as scouts, while the rest of the party began to make camp. Soon the sound of rifle fire made the whole group, save four left on guard at camp, remount, and, with their rifles at the ready, ride at a gallop toward the firing. After riding half a mile they came to an Indian village. Nearby, on a knoll, they could see their own men, protected by rocks, firing at two large detachments of Indians who were approaching from two directions and gradually spreading out to surround the knoll.

Charging directly through the line of advancing Indians, Frémont's men turned and drove them off. All of the expedition party got safely back to camp, keeping up a rear-guard fight with the Indians, who skulked along behind them, shouting threats all the way. That night a strong guard was kept at the camp, for it was obvious that the Indians were still about, waiting only for a moment when the white men were off guard in order to attack.

In the morning, camp broke early and the expedition pushed on. Riding ahead, Maxwell encountered a single Indian and fought a duel with him—the Indian using a bow and arrow, and Maxwell his pistols. When it was over, the Indian lay dead, Maxwell was untouched, and a Delaware had the attacking Indian's horse.

On January 15, 1846, the expedition was back at Sutter's Fort. Frémont went to San Francisco with eight men in Sutter's launch. He asked the Mexican commanding general, Don José Castro, for permission to continue his survey work in Mexican territory in order to lay out a convenient route from the United States to the Pacific.

He assured Castro that the object of his expedition was geographical and not military. Castro showed him every courtesy and readily granted the permission he asked, apparently in the greatest friendliness.

But on March 3, while the expedition was camped near Monterey, Lieutenant Chavez, a Mexican cavalry officer, accompanied by two other Mexican soldiers, galloped into the expedition's camp, bringing a peremptory order from Castro directing Frémont and his men to leave California at once. If the order was not obeyed promptly, the message said, military force would be used to bring about obedience.

Angered by Castro's breach of faith, and the brusque tone of the communication, Frémont told Chavez that he would not obey an order that was an insult to his government and to himself. Without further argument, the Mexican officer and his men wheeled their horses and rode away.

Early the next morning the Frémont expedition moved camp to the top of a small wooded flat called the Pic del Gabelano ("Peak of the Hawk") where wood and water, and grass for the animals, were plentiful, and from which the surrounding country could be observed for miles. Here the men quickly erected a rough but strong fort of solid logs and raised the American flag on a flagpole made from a straight sapling. During the short time they were there they could watch through spy glasses while Castro gathered his forces at a nearby mission. In addition to Mexicans, Indians were also being recruited, after having been given liquor to excite them.

On the second day a body of Mexican cavalry started up the road leading to the fortified camp, but stopped when a few hundred yards away, seemed to be holding a conference, and then turned back. On the third day the wind blew the flagpole over, and Frémont decided to make this an excuse for leaving the fort.

That night they camped a few miles from Pic del Gabelano, and about three miles from Castro's camp. A heavy guard stayed on duty all night, but the camp was not disturbed. Later Frémont learned that after the expedition had left the Pic, an Englishman named John Gilroy had ridden up the hill bearing a message from Castro, suggesting that he and Frémont meet and "make an arrangement." The arrangement that the Mexican general had in mind was, apparently, that he and Frémont join forces and together march against the Mexican Governor of California, Don Pio Pico.

Now, completely disregarding Castro's orders, Frémont went on with his exploring and surveying mission along the Bear River, and the Feather, a tributary of the Sacramento. The country through which he traveled was undulating and aglow with the gold of California poppies in bloom. So much did these please Frémont that later he gathered seeds from them to take back East with him.

While following the Sacramento River they found a great deal of game. One day, in a grove of oaks, they suddenly discovered they were in what Frémont described as "apparently a bear garden." The bears, resenting the intrusion of men, gave the hunters a lively time.

During the contest between bears and men the horse of
one of the Indians ("Delaware Charlie") fell, throwing
its rider. A bear charged at once, but immediately the
other hunters closed in and killed the beast before it
could reach its intended victim. After four bears had
been killed the others retreated. The only casualty was
Charlie's nose, which had been broken by a blow from
his gun as he fell from his horse.

Frémont reported:

We had no surgeon, but I managed to get it into good
shape and it healed without trace of injury. I was always
proud of this surgical operation, and the Delaware was
especially pleased. He was a fine-looking young man and
naïvely vain of his handsome face, which now had a nose
unusual among his people; the aquiline arch had been
broken to knit into a clear straight line, of which he became
very vain.

From March 3, when Castro had ordered Frémont
out of California, until early May he proceeded with his
surveying program without interruption. Then the march
of history caught up with him. The party was again at
Lake Klamath. One night, Frémont sat by the campfire
thinking of his former expedition when, at this place, the
Indian woman had ridden out to meet him beside her
husband, the chief, both expecting to be killed. Frémont
had liked both of them and hoped that he would be able
to find them and renew a friendly acquaintance.

His reverie was interrupted by the sound of horses'
hoofs, and in a moment two men were pulling their

horses to a halt in the circle of light cast by the fire. The two, whose names were Neal and Sigler, had ridden a hundred miles in two days to report that a United States officer named Gillespie was carrying important letters from Washington and trying to find Frémont. They had hurried ahead on better horses than Gillespie's because they were afraid that Gillespie might not be able to escape the Indians who, Neal said, were on his trail. The savages of this region were extremely warlike and considered all white men their enemies. Signs showed clearly that they were following Frémont's trail, and they had tried to cut off Neal and Sigler, but the two white men had evaded them.

Frémont's first thought was to go to Gillespie's aid. But it was night and he knew that the back trail along Lake Klamath could not be safely followed in the dark. So he quickly made arrangements for a party to leave at first light in the morning, and composed himself for the night.

At early dawn he took the trail with ten of his best men, including Carson, Lajeunesse, Owens, Stepp, Godey, and four of the Delawares. After a ride of about forty-five miles he ordered a halt by a river where he had camped before. He was sure that Gillespie would stop here, so he decided to wait.

The sun was going down when four white men rode out from behind the trees to be greeted by a shout of welcome. The leader was Lieutenant Archibald Gillespie of the Marine Corps. He had orders for Frémont from the War Department, as well as letters from home.

In Frémont's *Memoirs* the report of Gillespie's arrival and the exact nature of the orders he brought from Washington are vague, apparently purposely so. It is clear, however, that the orders absolved him from his duties as explorer, and placed upon him the responsibilities of an officer in the Army of the United States, who must now be prepared to fight, to defend himself and his men against attack, to learn as much as he could of the plans of other governments in California, to aid in thwarting any that might be an obstacle to the plan of the United States to make California its own, for this was now the chief object of the President. Letters from Senator Benton and others confirmed this view. Frémont commented:

I sat by the fire in fancied security, going over again the home letters. These threw their own light upon the communication from Mr. Gillespie and made the expected signal. In substance their effect was: The time has come. England must not get a foothold. We must be the first. Act; discreetly, but positively.

This meant more than a change in the plans of a peaceful expedition. This was war. This, he knew, was the beginning of the conquest of California, the first active stretching out of the powerful arm of the United States to draw a rich territory within the community of commonwealths that would determine much of the destiny of the western world.

The Fight with the Klamaths

✠

$\mathcal{P}$OLK'S intention, when he became President, was to buy California from Mexico, and thus acquire it peacefully. But the controversy over Texas prevented peaceful negotiations. Against the wishes of Mexico and Great Britain, but with the full support of the majority of Texans, the United States Congress had voted to admit the Republic of Texas to the Union as the twenty-eighth sovereign state. In bitter anger General Altamonte, the Mexican Minister to Washington, protested and left for Mexico. On March 24 the Mexican Minister of Foreign Affairs notified our minister that all diplomatic relations between the two countries were suspended. Seven thousand Mexican troops were massed on the south side of the Rio Grande, and Mexico warned Texas that the failure to accept Mexico's terms would be followed by invasion. The terms that Mexico proposed included a promise by the Republic of Texas that she would never annex herself to any other country. Texas promptly and unequivocally refused.

None of this was known to Frémont, of course, until Lieutenant Gillespie reached him at Lake Klamath. But we may be sure that the letters and orders the lieutenant carried included as many of the facts as were known when Gillespie left Washington. It was obvious now that the Texas problem, the California problem, and the Oregon problem were all related and that, in attempting to find a solution to one, all of them must be taken into account and acted upon decisively. Claims to all three territories by any power other than the United States of America must be vigorously opposed by whatever measures were necessary.

What could not have been included in Gillespie's dispatches was the fact that armed hostilities had actually begun between the United States and Mexico, when, on April 24, Mexican troops had attacked the troops of General Zachary Taylor on the Rio Grande, and been defeated by the Americans, and Colonel Stephen W. Kearny had been ordered to Santa Fe, to capture and garrison the town, and then proceed to upper California.

By the time Frémont had heard Gillespie's news and read the dispatches he carried, it was too late to start the return trip, so the men all camped where they were. During the night Frémont was awakened by Kit Carson's voice, calling to Basil and asking, "What's wrong over there?" The only answer was a groan. Immediately the camp was aroused by Kit and Owens who cried at the same time, "Indians! Indians!"

Hastening to where Basil Lajeunesse and a half-breed named Denny had slept, Frémont learned the terrible truth. Basil had been killed with a powerful axe blow that had split his head. The sound of the blow had awakened Kit and made him call out to Basil. Denny, whose dying groan had answered Kit's call, had been killed by arrows. In the flickering light of the campfire Frémont saw that the camp was under attack by a band of Klamath Indians.

All the Delawares but one named Crane had taken cover instantly at the sound of the warning from Kit and Owens. Crane had paused to fire the rifle he had picked up, but when he pulled the trigger a click indicated that it was not loaded. Only then did he discover that it was not his own rifle, and it was then too late to load it or to reach cover, for the Klamaths, after sending a flight of arrows, had charged, and several of them, led by their chief, were now closing in on him seeking to deliver a death blow. The valiant Delaware jumped nimbly from side to side, trying to evade their arrows and blows from their axes. Using his rifle as a club he fought bravely until, with five arrows in his body, he fell dead—but not before he had clubbed the chief to death. The two bodies lay almost touching each other, as the battle raged on. The rest of the party had meanwhile made frail barricades by hanging their blankets over the low branches of trees, or over bushes.

For some time the Indians tried to regain the body of their chief, but the rifle fire of the Frémont party prevented this, and finally they withdrew. For the rest of the night, however, none of the white men slept. All lay behind their fragile cover, their cocked rifles in their hands, watching, and waiting for a renewed attack.

When daylight came they saw that all of the living

Night assault by the Indians

Indians had disappeared. Only the dead chief lay there beside the body of Crane and near the bodies of Basil and Denny as evidence of the bloody work that had been done the night before. Still attached to the waist of the chief was an English hatchet. Frémont recognized the dead man as one to whom he had given food and presents for his tribe. In the dead chief's quiver were forty arrows, of which Carson said, "They are the most beautiful and warlike arrows I have ever seen." Each was tipped with a needle-sharp piece of iron, and poisoned for six inches above the point.

After packing the bodies of their own dead on mules, and leaving the dead chief where he lay, the party started back toward their main camp. As they made their way along Lake Klamath, which, at this time of year, was filled with water, a number of canoes appeared, all heading for a point where the trail came down to the shore. A prolonged cry like that of a loon indicated to Frémont and Carson that a scout was giving the Indians a warning of the approach of the white men.

Frémont knew that the bodies of Basil, Denny, and Crane would be an impediment in case of a fight, so he turned off the trail into a laurel thicket where the men dug a shallow grave with their knives. "There are men above whom the laurels bloom who did not better deserve them than my brave Delaware and Basil," Frémont wrote later. "I left Denny's name on the creek where he died."

Apparently the party's leaving the trail disconcerted the Indians and upset the plan for an ambush at the lake for, when the white men returned to the trail along the lake, all of the canoes had disappeared. Frémont's party reached the main camp that afternoon. That night all the Delawares blackened their faces in mourning, as Frémont expressed his sympathy and his own sense of loss, voicing his admiration for the bravery and general worthiness of Crane.

Frémont knew that some of the Klamaths in the band that had killed the three men had followed the party back to the camp and were now lurking in the vicinity. With this in mind he and Swanok planned an ambush of their own. In the morning all left the camp and rode a few hundred yards. There the Delawares left their horses and, taking cover, found their way on foot back to the campsite secretly while the others waited, knowing that the Klamaths would come into camp, to see if anything had been left behind, as soon as it had been vacated. In a few minutes the sound of rifle fire was heard, and almost immediately the Delawares returned, with Swanok in the lead, carrying two bloody scalps.

The route continued along the lake and, as before, the many canoes they saw showed that the Indians were still in an aggressive mood. The next day Frémont sent Carson and Owens ahead with ten men to reconnoiter. There was an Indian fishing village, Frémont knew, not far off on a river that emptied into Lake Klamath. Soon the sound of rifle fire made the main party dash ahead with rifles at the ready. As they neared the lake Frémont saw a dead Indian sitting in the stern of a canoe, wearing shoes that he was quite sure Lajeunesse had been wearing when he was killed. Kit, Owens, and the ten other scouts were on the opposite bank of the river. Fortunately the stream could be forded at this spot, and the horses of the white men dashed in and across under a hail of arrows, none of which took effect. They found that the Indians had left their village and had taken a stand behind an expanse of sagebrush, each with his arrows spread out before him in a fan shape, so that they could be taken up and fitted to the bow string quickly.

Fourteen of the Indians were killed, without any losses among their attackers, before the Indians finally gave up and ran off. Frémont's men then burned the reed huts of the village and destroyed quantities of fish and the scaffolding on which they were drying.

As the party went on they encountered a lone Indian of unusual courage who made a stand by himself. He was about to shoot Carson, when Kit raised his rifle and pulled the trigger. But there was only a click, as the gun refused to fire, and Kit quickly threw himself to one side to avoid the Indian's arrow. At the same time Frémont fired, and missed. As the Indian, still standing bravely without any cover, was fitting another arrow to his bow, Frémont's horse, Sacramento, saved the day. Guided by Frémont he simply ran the Indian down, knocking him over and jumping across the fallen body. Sagundai, who was behind Frémont, quickly leaped from his horse and killed the Klamath with his war club.

The score was now seventeen to three, and Frémont hoped that the Klamaths had learned a lesson and that there would be no more trouble. He wrote:

I had now kept the promise I made to myself and had punished these people well for their treachery. . . . When the Tlamaths tell the story of the night attack . . . there will be no boasting. They will have to tell also of the death of their chief and of our swift retaliation; and how the people at the fishery had to mourn for the loss of their men and the destruction of their village.

In spite of the fact that the Klamaths were waging a losing battle, there were two more encounters with them. One was between Maxwell and Archambeau and a lone Indian. The Klamath fired at Maxwell without warning. Maxwell, seeing the action just as the Indian let the bow string go, flung himself from his horse in time to evade the arrow, and shot the Indian dead with his rifle. The other occurred a few days later when a band attacked the entire Frémont party. All were quickly driven off but one, well protected by a rock, who refused to leave but kept discharging arrows until Carson managed to work his way around to the back of the rock and shot him through the heart.

There had been some trouble with the Klamaths before, but nothing that compared with the savagery and persistence of these recent attacks. It was as though the Indians were determined to wipe the entire Frémont party out, no matter how many of their own men they lost in the process. Why? Frémont thought he knew.

On May 24 he wrote to Senator Benton. It was what the explorer himself called a "guarded letter," yet, while there was no direct accusation in it, the meaning seems clear. First he told the story of the attacks. Then:

Tlamath Lake . . . the heart of the Tlamath nation. . . . Directly west, and comparatively near at hand, is the Umpqua River. *Here the British have a post.* Why do they keep it there? The fur trade will not justify it. If there is to be any war with England, it is of great importance that they should instantly be driven from this and similar posts before they furnish the Indians with firearms, and engage them in their service. These Indians are considered by the Willamette missionaries . . . as the most savage and warlike Indians on the continent. . . . This post maintains an intercourse with the Tlamaths and other mountain Indians, and furnishes them with the tomahawks and iron arrowheads with which they fought us. They are the bravest Indians we have ever seen; our people (my camp, Carson, etc.) consider them far beyond the Blackfeet, who are by no means so daring. You know that the Indians along the line of the Columbia are well supplied with firearms, ammunition, and horses— hardly a man having less than forty or fifty of the latter— that they are brave, friendly to the British, and unfriendly

Lake Klamath

to us. These things may be worthy of Mr. Buchanan's attention. [James Buchanan was Secretary of State.]

While he was at Neal's ranch on the Sacramento, several settlers came to Frémont appealing to him for protection from the Indians who were leaving their homes and taking to the mountains. These and other signs indicated that they were preparing for systematic warfare against the whites. This was confirmed by a messenger from Captain Sutter who warned Frémont that Castro had sent men among the Indian tribes, rousing them to battle. If, then, both the British and the Mexicans were inciting the Indians to war and using them as their tools, the situation was indeed serious. In spite of Frémont's friendliness to the peaceful Indians, and his sympathy for them as they were gradually being deprived of their freedom, he had good reason to know what dangerous foes they could be, and he was not unmindful of his responsibility to the white settlers as well. He wrote:

An Indian let loose is of all animals the most savage. He has an imagination for devilment that seems peculiar to him, and a singular delight in inflicting suffering. I had once come upon a scene where a band of savages had had their own way—no relief could come, as they thought—the men had been killed and mutilated—the women pinned to the ground by stakes driven through their bodies, while yet alive. Bearing this in mind I resolved there should be no such scenes here—no more men skinned alive—no more women impaled—and I told the men to take their families home and have them rest in quiet; I would take charge of the Indians and they might surely rely on me not to leave the valley while there was any danger.

He now planned a decisive action that would make the Indians realize, as he put it, that "Castro was far and I was near." A number of Indian villages were strung out along the western bank of the Sacramento. He decided to strike them all suddenly and hard. Early one morning he set out with most of his men. At the first village they saw that the Indian men had feathers in their hair and black paint on their faces, which meant preparation for war. Frémont's men killed a number of Indians and scattered the rest, many of whom leaped into the river and swam to the other side. The news spread rapidly so that in most of the other villages Frémont and his men found only barking dogs, half-wild, ragged ponies, and men escaping—usually by swimming the river, their heads dotting the surface of the stream like floating corks.

The engagements with the Klamaths were not the sort of battles that become immortalized in books of history. But Frémont knew they were part of a larger event that would be of great importance to the United States and to the world. Now the war with Mexico was being fought not only along the Rio Grande, but also in upper California. The conquest of what was later to be known as "the golden state" was under way. The problems of Texas, California, and Oregon were about to be settled, and when the war was over the Stars and Stripes would fly undisputed from the Atlantic to the Pacific.

The Bear Flag War and
the Conquest of California

✠

RÉMONT now knew that he was in a position requiring the greatest caution and wisdom. His orders from Washington were vague and general. He was to proceed "with firmness and with discretion," but proceed to do what? He was to further the purpose of the United States to annex California, but was he to further it to the extent of engaging in armed warfare with the Mexicans? He did not know that Congress had already declared war on Mexico, and, unwilling to place the United States in an embarrassing position by taking unauthorized aggressive action, he decided to play a waiting game, while aiding others who were more impulsive.

The "others" were settlers in California from the United States who were becoming daily more impatient with the aggressive acts of the Mexicans and of the Indians, inspired by the Mexicans. A number of these settlers had come to Frémont's camp and reported that Castro had ordered all Americans who had not become Mexican citizens to leave California at once, and had threatened to drive out by force those who did not go willingly. It was also rumored that the Mexican general was gathering a force for this very purpose, and stirring up the Indians to destroy the crops of the Americans. If some of the Americans were destroyed with the crops —well, no matter, they had been warned.

Actually none of these stories was true, but they were believed to be. When it was learned that a band of one hundred and fifty horses, collected at Sonoma, were on their way to Castro, a number of armed settlers set off to intercept them, and in forty-eight hours returned with the horses which they had seized from Castro's men. This, they were sure, would bring about retaliation by Castro, so the same group, enlisting others to aid them, returned to Sonoma under the leadership of William B. Ide, an enterprising Vermonter. They entered the town on June 14 and, in a surprise attack, captured it and took some high Mexican officials as prisoners, who were sent under guard to Frémont.

But Frémont was not yet ready to take an active part in armed aggression against Mexico. Saying that he had nothing to do with the affair, he sent the prisoners to Sutter's Fort where they were locked up in the jail. This caused a bitter quarrel between Frémont and Sutter, in which Sutter was warned that if he did not cooperate with the Americans he would be ejected from the fort by force. Later the two men seemed to be friends, but in effect Sutter was no longer in control of his fort.

Meanwhile Ide and his rag-tag rebel force announced at Sonoma that they were founding a new republic. Among them was William L. Todd, a nephew of Mrs. Abraham Lincoln, who made a flag of a piece of whitish-brown cloth a yard and a half long. On its upper right-hand corner he placed a large star and, facing it, the figure of what he intended to be a bear, but which looked so much like a pig that native Californians called it "the shoat." Below the star and the bear, spreading across the length of the flag, he painted the words "California Republic." Ide pulled down the Mexican flag and raised the flag made by Todd. Ide now published a proclamation guaranteeing peace and security to all who would not bear arms against the forces of the "California Republic," which had been formed, the proclamation said, to overthrow a selfish, incompetent government. This engagement became known as "the bear flag war."

As soon as Castro heard of the taking of Sonoma he sent a force under Joaquin de la Torre to retake it. The bear-flag men immediately sent word to Frémont asking him to come to their aid, and Frémont decided that "it was for me rather to govern events than to be governed by them."

Yet his position was still an uncertain one. With no regular army force in the Far West, authority was vested in Commodore John D. Sloat, Commander-in-Chief of U.S. Naval Forces in the Pacific. Sloat was, at this time, in his flagship, the *Savannah,* anchored off Monterey. With him were two sloops of war, the *Cyane* and the *Levant.* Frémont would have been justified in communicating with Sloat to ask him for orders, had he been unwilling to take responsibility for direct action. Instead he made plans to aid the garrison at Sonoma.

But his uncertainty as to whether he was actually

Top: The Bear Guidon that belonged to the Sonoma troop of the California Battalion; Bottom: The original Bear Flag. Both passed into the possession of the San Francisco Society of California Pioneers

carrying out the intent of his instructions from Washington, and his unwillingness to embarrass the United States government, if he was not, are indicated by the fact that, before leaving, he wrote his resignation and a letter to Senator Benton, asking him to deliver the resignation to the Secretary of War in case the Army did not want to be held responsible for what he (Frémont) had done. Then he hurried to Sonoma, joined the revolutionists, and was made their commander.

On July 5, while still at Sonoma, Frémont wrote Captain Montgomery who was aboard the *Portsmouth,* reporting that "a military organization of the force under arms was made yesterday at this place," and added, "foreigners from below are daily arriving at this post and . . . upwards of a hundred good men are now in the upper part of the Sacramento Valley . . ."

Though engaged in warlike activities, Frémont still found time and inclination to indulge in the poetic fancy that was a part of his nature. Undoubtedly impressed by the spectacle of the setting sun spilling its light like liquid gold between the two hills that guard the narrow entrance to San Francisco Bay he gave the passage the name that has become famous, "The Golden Gate."

Though there was still no official U.S. Army force in California, an effective army, under Frémont, was growing day by day. He now had 234 men in four companies, called "the California Battalion." Lieutenant Gillespie worked closely with him and under him, and he had made Ezekiel Merritt his field aide. Merritt was a tall, thin, rugged settler, fearless and clever, who acted promptly on order without asking questions. Kern, too, who had come with the expedition as a topographer, was proving capable as a member of the military force.

Leaving a detachment at Sonoma, Frémont returned to the American Fork where his main camp was located near Sutter's Fort. Here a messenger from Commodore Sloat brought the news that war existed between the United States and Mexico, that Sloat had taken Monterey and raised the United States flag over it, that Commodore John B. Montgomery had taken Yerba Buena (the settlement that grew to be San Francisco), and that Sloat requested Frémont to join him with a hundred men at Monterey as soon as possible.

With the messenger came a United States flag that Frémont raised at once over Sutter's Fort to a salute of twenty-one guns, and a proclamation that Frémont read aloud at the flag-raising ceremony. In it Sloat claimed California as a part of the United States, called upon Castro to surrender, and assured the people of all the rights of United States citizens. Because Sutter was an officer in the Mexican army, Frémont placed Edward Kern in charge of Sutter's Fort. He then started marching to Monterey with his battalion.

An excellent description of Frémont by William D. Phelps, who met him during the days of the California adventure, was quoted in the New York *Tribune* on August 14, 1856.

". . . a slender and well-proportioned man, of sedate but pleasing countenance. . . . His dress, as near as I can remember, was a blue flannel shirt, after the naval style, open at the collar, which was turned over; over this a deerskin hunting shirt, figured and trimmed in hunter's style, blue cloth pantaloons and neat moccasins. His head was not cumbered by hat or cap of any shape, but a light cotton handkerchief, bound tightly around his head, surmounted a suit which might not appear very fashionable at the White House or be presentable at the Queen's levee; but to my eye it was an admirable rig to scud under or fight in.

On his way to Monterey, Frémont took possession of San Juan and, passing the Pic del Gabelano, which he had held for three days, all of the men saluted the peak.

At Monterey, Frémont found that an English battleship, the *Collingwood*, under Rear Admiral Sir George Seymour, had joined the American ships, and learned later that the seamen on the three American ships in the harbor had all gone to their battle stations and prepared for action when the British vessel hove into sight. But no action was necessary. One of the officers on the *Collingwood*, Lieutenant Frederick Walpole, wrote a description of Frémont's entry into Monterey with his men.

Here were true trappers, the class that produced the heroes of Fenimore Cooper's best works. . . . A vast cloud of dust appeared first, and thence in long file emerged this wildest wild party. Frémont rode ahead, a spare, active looking man. . . . He was dressed in a blouse and leggings, and wore a felt hat. After him came five Delaware Indians, who were his bodyguard. . . . The rest, many of them blacker than the Indians, rode two by two, the rifle held by one hand across the pommel of the saddle. . . . The dress of these men was principally a long loose coat of deerskin, tied with thongs in front; trowsers of the same, of their own manufacture. They are allowed no liquor, tea and sugar only; this, no doubt, has much to do with their good conduct; and the discipline, too, is very strict. . . . The butts of the trappers' rifles resemble a Turkish musket, therefore fit light to the shoulder; they are very long and very heavy, carry ball about thirty-eight to the pound.

Frémont camped between Monterey and the sea on a flat among firs and pines. As soon as the camp was established, he reported to Commodore Sloat on board the *Savannah,* taking Lieutenant Gillespie with him. And now the situation that had plagued him from the beginning of his activities as captain of a combat force—the vagueness of his orders—caused embarrassment between him and the Commodore.

The Commodore asked Frémont under what authority he had acted, and was told that Frémont had proceeded on his own responsibility and without any express authority from the government to engage in hostilities. This greatly disturbed Sloat, who now felt that he had probably been unjustified in raising the flag of the United States over Monterey. (Later Secretary of the Navy George Bancroft mildly censured the Commodore—not for having raised the United States flag over Monterey, but for his long delay in taking action.) Frémont wrote of the interview, in part:

. . . the interview terminated abruptly. . . . He did not ask me for another. . . . Naturally I was surprised by the result. . . . I had returned to California with my mind full of one purpose. . . . I saw the lovely country which had charmed my senses with admiration for its beauty dangerously near to becoming the appendage of a foreign power. I knew that the men who understood the future of our country, and who at this time ruled its destinies and were the government, regarded the California coast as the boundary fixed by nature to round off our natural domain . . .

Returning to the shore from my visit to the *Savannah,* I walked out toward the Point of Pines which juts into the sea. No matter how untoward this interview had been I felt that the die was cast . . .

Shortly after Frémont's unsatisfactory interview with Sloat, the latter, who was ill, turned his command over to Commodore R. F. Stockton, who suggested to Frémont that he and all of the men in his battalion volunteer to serve under Stockton's command, adding that in this case a naval battalion on land would be formed, with Frémont as major, and Gillespie as captain. Godey was made a lieutenant. (Before the conquest of California had been completed Frémont was made a lieutenant colonel.) The Pathfinder and his men accepted and placed themselves without reservation under Stockton's authority. Frémont thus lost much of the freedom of action he had had in his former status, but also placed himself in a much more definite position in regard to any action that might be taken. The responsibility was now Commodore Stockton's.

Following Stockton's orders, Frémont and his force now went to San Diego by ship, and from there marched to a point near Los Angeles, where he was joined by the Commodore. The combined forces marched into the town and took it without opposition.

General Castro meanwhile had broken up his camp nearby, buried much of his armament, and dispersed his forces. Castro himself had fled to a mountain overlooking the San Gabriel plain, and the Mexican governor of California, Don Pio Pico, had retired to one of his estates about forty miles south of Los Angeles.

In August, Commodore Stockton organized a civil government, formally indicating that California was now a part of the United States. Frémont was appointed military governor and Gillespie commandant of the southern district.

Frémont wrote a report of all these events for Secretary of the Navy Bancroft. He sent Kit Carson, with an escort of sixteen men, to Washington with the report and some personal letters. Then Frémont left to go to the Sacramento Valley on Stockton's orders to recruit as many men as possible. It was Stockton's plan at this time to proceed against Acapulco or Mazatlan and from there to fight his way to Mexico City, or as close to it as possible.

But several local rebellions delayed the start for Mexico. The situation was especially serious in Southern California where a number of Californians revolted against the American proclamation and, under the leadership of Captain José Maria Flores, retook Los Angeles, and set up a government with Flores as Governor and Commander-in-Chief.

Then came the big surprise. On December 3 Commodore Stockton received a letter from Brigadier General Kearny saying that he had completed the conquest of New Mexico, was now in California, to which he had come "by orders from the President of the United States," and asking Stockton to send a guide so that the two could meet. Stockton immediately sent Gillespie with a field piece and a detachment of mounted riflemen, including Godey, among others.

Gillespie had no difficulty finding Kearny, and the combined forces set out at once for the attack. On their way to Los Angeles they defeated a detachment of Mexican soldiers in bloody fighting at San Pascual. But at San Bernardino they were forced to take a defensive position while three men set off for San Diego at night to obtain aid. Stockton at once sent a force of two hundred marines and sailors. At dawn on the eleventh of December these, with Kearny's and Gillespie's men, entered San Diego without opposition, for the enemy had disappeared at the sight of the superior force. On the eighth and ninth of January the last two fights between the Americans and the Californians took place and Los Angeles was taken. The Californians surrendered to Frémont, who, on his way to Los Angeles with four hundred men, was about thirty miles from his destination when the surrender party met him. The military conquest of California was complete.

Conflict with Kearny
and Court Martial

✠

WHEN FRÉMONT next saw Godey he was amazed to learn that Carson, who had been sent to Washington, was actually with Kearny. What had happened, he learned later, was this: Some eight hundred miles east of Los Angeles, Kit, hurrying eastward along the Rio Grande on his mission to Washington, had met Kearny moving westward toward California with his three hundred dragoons. Kit had told the Brigadier General that the conquest of California was virtually completed and that there was no need to go there. The General then decided to send all but a hundred of his dragoons back, but to continue to California with the others, and ordered Carson to go along with him as guide. Carson's protests were unheeded; the dispatches to Washington were sent on by another courier. Kit, who had looked forward to seeing his people and to visiting the nation's capital, turned his face westward again.

The first time that Frémont met Kearny and Stockton together he saw that the two men were obviously on a collision course. He wrote of it in a letter to Senator Benton after the surrender of the Mexican army.

When I entered Los Angeles I was ignorant of the relations subsisting between these gentlemen, having received from neither any order or information which might serve as a guide in the circumstances. I therefore, immediately on my arrival, waited upon the governor and commander in chief, Commodore Stockton; and a few minutes afterwards, called on General Kearny. I soon found them occupying a hostile attitude, and each denying the right of the other to assume direction of affairs in this country.

The ground assumed by General Kearny was that he held in his hand plenary instructions from the President directing him to conquer California, and organize a civil government, and that consequently he would not recognize the acts of Commodore Stockton.

The latter maintained that his own instructions were to the same effect as Kearny's; that his [Kearny's] officer's commission was obsolete, and never would have been given could the government have anticipated that the entire country, seaboard, and interior, would have been conquered and held by himself. . . . His work had been anticipated; his commission was absolutely void, null, and of no effect.

Though two men less headstrong and willful than Kearny and Stockton would probably have found a way to compromise their differences without bitterness, each had some justification for his stand in the orders that he had received from Washington. Those sent to the naval commander in the Pacific by the Secretary of the Navy, under which Stockton claimed authority, justified him in authorizing Frémont to organize the California Battalion and to take orders from him. Kearny was apparently in much the same position, having had similar orders from the Secretary of War. Frémont was in the position of a subordinate officer, loyal to Stockton, the man under whom he had volunteered to serve. He was caught in the cross fire between two opposing duelists.

The showdown between Kearny and Frémont was to come very quickly. On January 16, 1847, Frémont received the following note from Lieutenant William F. Emory, acting assistant adjutant general to General Kearny:

By direction of Brigadier General Kearny I send you a copy of a communication to him from the Secretary of War, dated June 18, 1846, in which is the following, "These troops and such as may be organized in California will be under your comand." The general directs that no change be made in the organization of your battalion of volunteers or officers appointed to it, without his sanction or approval being first obtained.

There was an immediate issue at stake. When Frémont had accepted Stockton's appointment as military governor of California, he had created a vacancy in the leadership of his battalion. His replacement as commander and other changes had become necessary. Also Stockton had ordered that as many men as possible be recruited to join the battalion. These were the acts that Kearny now forbade.

Knowing the firm stand that Stockton had taken in the matter, and realizing that his own acceptance of Stockton as his superior officer placed a definite responsibility upon him, Frémont felt that if he obeyed Kearny's order he would actually be guilty of disobedience to Stockton, whose authority he had already accepted. Undoubtedly, there was also an element of personal loyalty to Stockton in the difficult decision that Frémont made. He made quite clear on which side he stood in the letter that he wrote to Kearny in answer to Emory's letter.

After reviewing the circumstances under which he had voluntarily submitted himself to Stockton's authority, he ended his letter with a declaration devoid of subterfuge or even of tact:

I feel, therefore, with great deference to your professional and personal character, constrained to say that, until you and Commodore Stockton adjust between yourselves the question of rank, where I respectfully think the difference belongs, I shall have to report and receive orders, as heretofore, from the commodore.

As the conflict for the control of the army and civil government in the newly acquired territory of California grew increasingly bitter, the position of Lieutenant Colonel Frémont became more difficult, for much of Kearny's resentment against Stockton seemed to find expression in abuse of Frémont. Perhaps it was because the lieutenant colonel was of a lower rank than the Commodore, or because a general of the army resented having an army command take orders from the navy, or because Kearny knew that the letter Frémont had written him refusing to accept his authority was a powerful weapon, as he later proved.

Events moved rapidly through the late winter months and the spring of 1847. On the day that Emory wrote Frémont demanding that he submit any changes he planned to make to Kearny for approval, Kearny wrote Stockton demanding "that you cease all further proceedings relating to the formation of a civil government for this territory, as I cannot recognize in you any right in assuming to perform duties confided to me by the President." The next day Stockton wrote Kearny saying, "I cannot do anything nor desist from anything on your demand, which I will submit to the President and ask for your recall. In the meantime you will consider yourself suspended from the command of the United States forces in this place."

Following this verbal broadside, Kearny apparently decided to rest on his arms for the moment, writing Stockton, "I must, for the purpose of preventing a collision between us and probably a civil war in consequence of it, remain silent for the present, leaving with you the great responsibility of doing that for which you have no authority, and preventing me from complying with the President's orders."

So matters rested without any agreement having been reached until, early in the spring of 1847, Commodore Stockton received a communication from the Secre-

Brigadier General Philip Kearny

tary of the Navy ordering him to turn over to General Kearny the entire control of operations on land and "the administrative functions of the government over the people and territory occupied by us." Kearny received orders confirming his authority from W. L. Marcy, Secretary of War, which included instructions to give Frémont his choice between returning to the United States or staying and serving under Kearny.

But when Frémont applied, first for permission to join General Taylor's command in Mexico, and later, to return to the United States, both requests were denied. Instead he was placed under Colonel R. R. Mason, whom Kearny had made commander of the southern district. Mason treated Frémont with such contempt that on April 14, the latter, in a flaming rage, considering one of Mason's orders an insult, challenged his superior officer to a duel. Fortunately "the meeting," as such encounters were then called, was postponed several times, and finally was forbidden by General Kearny.

On June 14, Kearny broke camp near Sutter's Fort and, ordering Frémont to accompany him, started eastward. At the very beginning of the march Frémont was ordered to march at the rear and subjected to other indignities. The climax came on August 22 at Fort Leavenworth when Kearny summoned Frémont and directed Lieutenant Wharton to read to him the first paragraph of an order the General had issued on that day. Frémont stood in shocked and incredulous silence as he learned that he was under arrest on three charges: Mutiny (an offense for which the penalty was death); Disobedience of the Lawful Command of a Superior Officer; and Conduct to the Prejudice of Good Order and Discipline. All three charges were based on the final sentence in the letter Frémont had written General Kearny on January 17, in which he rejected Kearny's authority and announced that he would report to and take orders from Commodore Stockton. He was now ordered to proceed at once to Washington and report to the Adjutant General of the Army.

Consequently, Frémont and his persecutor separated, and Frémont sadly and angrily hurried along the old familiar trail, which he had followed both eastward and westward several times. But this time a tremendous surprise was waiting for him. As he reached Kansas Landing, a boat from St. Louis was just pulling in and being made fast to the dock, just in fine time, he thought, to take him to St. Louis. He pushed through the crowd of loafers, lounging about the landing, toward the lowered gangplank. Suddenly he heard a gasping cry of surprise and joy and, looking up, saw Jessie running down the gangplank. She threw herself into his arms with tears of happiness running down her cheeks. For more than two years they had been separated. Now the joy of their reunion made the cloud of depression that hung over both of them lift for a little while.

News of Frémont's troubles with Kearny and his return under arrest had preceded him and reached Jessie in St. Louis. She had immediately hurried to Kansas Landing, intending to wait there until he arrived. By the merest chance the timing had been perfect.

As their boat proceeded down the river, crowds thronged the docks to cheer. At St. Louis a great gathering at the landing stage gave him a tumultuous welcome, and he addressed them briefly. A number of distinguished citizens called on him to ask permission to arrange an elaborate public dinner in his honor. But Frémont felt that until his name had been cleared such a celebration would be inappropriate and declined with thanks. However it was clear that, to the public, he was returning, not in disgrace, but as a hero who had covered himself with glory. Surely his arrest had been a mistake, and soon the matter would be cleared up and could be forgotten.

Pausing only briefly in St. Louis, Frémont and Jessie hurried on to Washington, reaching the capital about

September 16. He at once reported to the Adjutant General and demanded a trial by Court Martial.

But the calamity of Kearny's damning charges against him was compounded by a personal sorrow that caused him to ask for a short leave of absence and a postponement of his trial until he could fulfill another personal duty. Upon reaching home he learned that the news of his arrest had reached his mother in Aiken, South Carolina and that she was dangerously ill. Having received the leave of absence, Frémont hastened south, but reached Aiken too late, for his mother died a few hours before he arrived. The next day he accompanied her body to Charleston for burial, and then hurried back to Washington.

Before he left Charleston Frémont learned that his admirers in South Carolina had raised money by popular subscription with which to present a memorial sword to him, and that the ladies of Charleston had added a suitable belt to the gift. In view of his mother's death, the presentation ceremonies were postponed. The presentation was made later, soon after the opening of Congress, by representatives of South Carolina.

The sword was a splendid piece of workmanship, with silver and gold mountings. The head of the hilt was fashioned to resemble the summit of a palmetto tree. Around it was coiled the figure of a rattlesnake, a part of the old arms of the state. On the guard was a map, with a part of the word "Oregon" visible. On the gold scabbard were engraved "California," and "1846," and below these the following inscription:

FRÉMONT

Presented
By the citizens of Charleston
To LIEUTENANT-COLONEL
JOHN CHARLES FRÉMONT
A Memorial of their High Appreciation
of the Gallantry and Science
He has Displayed in His
Services in Oregon and California

Below the inscription was engraved a representation of a buffalo hunt.

The General Court Martial began on November 2, 1847 and lasted until January 31, 1848. Frémont's father-in-law, Senator Benton, and his brother-in-law, William Carey Jones, were appointed to conduct his defense. Actually the defendant seems pretty much to have defended himself, for there is on a record an eloquent address to the court, justifying his actions. It consists of some forty thousand words. The reading of it consumed three sessions of the court. In it Frémont logically demolished all of the charges made by General Kearny.

The newspapers treated the trial as the most important news story of the times, giving columns of space to it day after day, and, in general, showing Frémont in a favorable light. It was clear that the sympathy of the press and public was with Frémont, and that the very coverage of the trial in the press increased the nation's respect and affection for the man who had contributed more than any other one person to the winning of the West and the conquest of California. Before the trial

Frémont had been only a name to many Americans. Now, throughout the nation, he was being publicized as a national hero.

The trial and details of the evidence were among the chief subjects of conversation in official Washington during the weeks when the issue remained in doubt. The consensus in the capital was that Frémont should, and would, be cleared. Many old army hands declared that, in Frémont's position, they would have found it immensely difficult to decide whether authority was vested in Stockton or in Kearny, and that they would have done exactly as Frémont had done.

After Frémont had rested his case, the court took three days in which to deliberate and then, in a decision that surprised and shocked a number of people, returned a verdict of "Guilty" on all three counts, and sentenced Frémont to dismissal from the service. Six of the ten members of the court, however, recommended the accused to the lenient consideration and clemency of the President. When the verdict was announced, many observers intimated that it was merely an example of the low opinion West Pointers always had of an outsider. The New York *Herald* said this, in effect, calling Frémont "a greater, though a younger, man than a majority of his triers."

The ways of the legal mind are strange, and nowhere more so than in military Court Martial procedures. To the strangeness of this combination of condemnation and recommendation for clemency President Polk's action added still greater confusion. He refused to confirm the verdict as to the charge of mutiny, but "approved" the sentence, which, however, he immediately remitted, ordered Frémont to be released from arrest, directed that his sword be returned to him, and instructed Frémont himself to return to duty. Thus matters were as they had been before, save that there was a stain on the Pathfinder's name that he felt was unjust.

In view of this injustice and the fact that, as he himself put it in a letter to the Adjutant General of the Army, he did "not feel conscious of having done anything to merit the finding of the court," he refused to accept the clemency of the President, which he felt would be to acknowledge the justice of the verdict against him, and resigned from the army.

Later that year Kearny died in St. Louis. From his deathbed he sent his physician to ask Jessie to come to see him. It seemed obvious that, in his last hours, he wanted to find a way to become reconciled with her husband. But the proud Jessie declined his invitation, and the General died with the probably unhappy memory of his attempt to discredit one of America's most illustrious heroes.

Death in the Snow

✠

ON JULY 14, 1848, a second child, a boy, to whom the name Benton was given, was born to the Frémonts. He was a frail child, and died less than three months later while the Frémont family were on a steamer on the Missouri River.

For Frémont was going west again—this time with his whole family. The trip had a double purpose. Before starting east from California to face his Court Martial trial, he had left with Thomas O. Larkin, who had been the American Consul to California when it had been under Mexican rule, $3,000 with which to buy a ranch. He had specified a property he himself had picked out in the hills near San Francisco. Here he intended to make his home, and hoped to combine farming with the practice of law. Friends in the East had lent him money with which he had bought agricultural implements and machinery for a mill, all of which were being shipped by sea around Cape Horn.

But the purpose of their trip was not merely to go to a new home. Nor were they going all of the way together. Jessie was to travel with her husband only as far as Westport Landing (originally Kansas Landing, and now Kansas City) on the Missouri River. Here Frémont was to leave her and start overland on the Santa Fe Trail in command of a fourth expedition which he had organized and would command. It would be quite independent of the army or any other department of government. This was to be Frémont's own venture, in a way in which none of the others had been. He hoped to find a more southerly route across the Rockies than any yet known, which would, he hoped, intersect the head of the Rio Grande.

Jessie, meanwhile, was to go back, cross the Isthmus of Panama, and take a boat from there to San Francisco, where Frémont was to meet her at the end of his arduous journey.

This fourth expedition was an expression of Frémont's eternal curiosity and love of adventure. It also was, in a sense, almost a gesture of defiance against the verdict of the Court Martial. It was as though he were saying to the world, "I am the explorer Frémont. I am the Pathfinder. Nothing that a Court Martial can say about me will change my place in the history of the West."

But there was, in addition, a less personal and most important motive. Following the excitement that reports of his earlier expeditions had created, the desire for a railroad that would cross the continent was growing in the minds of forward-looking men. One of the oft-recurring questions in connection with discussions of the revolutionary idea was whether or not snow on the

Rockies would make such a project impossible. Frémont decided to cross the Great Divide in winter to find the answer. The record is not completely clear as to the financing of the expedition, but apparently a wealthy group in St. Louis, interested in the railroad project, did so, at least in part.

At Westport Landing, Frémont bade his wife goodby and set forth with his expedition. Jessie and "Aunt Kitty," her maid, stayed that night in quarters provided by the Indian Agency at Westport. It was almost dawn when they were disturbed by the sound of galloping hoofs. With typical impetuousness, Frémont had ridden back ten miles from the first encampment of his fourth expedition, for another good-by to his wife. "And so," as Jessie reported the episode, "with our early tea for a stirrup cup, 'he gave his bridle rein a shake' and we went our ways, one into the midwinter snows of untracked mountains, the other to the long sea voyage through the tropics."

The expedition, which started confidently westward from Westport Landing, consisted of thirty-three men with horses and pack animals. Some of the old bunch were there—Preuss and Alexander Godey, both of whom had braved the winter passage across the Sierras with Frémont. King was also in the company, and Kern, with two brothers, one of whom was a physician. Among the new men were Captain Cathcart of the British Army and Micajah McGehee, who had a wide reputation as a frontiersman. For some reason that Frémont does not explain in his notes, Kit Carson, now living at Taos, did not join him on this expedition. In Kit's place Frémont engaged at Pueblo a guide known as "Old Bill" Williams, an expert scout and mountain man.

On November 26, 1848, the party entered the Rockies at a point southwest of Pueblo. Before them rose the awesome frozen cliffs and snow-covered peaks that their leader was determined to cross at any cost. Day by day their difficulties increased as the icy and often sleet-laden blasts seemed to be trying to force them back over the rocky, treacherous ground which they had conquered at great effort. There were frozen hands, ears, and toes. The only food for the animals was dry grain which they carried into the mountains; the only water was melted snow. With every step upward the cold increased until no thermometer the expedition carried was capable of registering it. A number of the mules froze to death and their bodies were left behind to be quickly covered by the drifting snow.

They crossed one range and came down on the other side into the San Luis Valley, which itself was 7,000 feet above sea level, and to the Rio Grande, which normally would have been a rushing torrent, so swift was its descent at this point. But now it was frozen over from bank to bank. Above them rose another range—the San Juan—with peaks 14,000 feet above sea level. Here Frémont and Bill Williams disagreed about the best route, but finally the party took the route recommended by Williams, through the so-called Carnero Pass. It was now the 8th of December, and the cold was intense.

For nine days the group struggled on, suffering bitterly, watching their animals die one by one, feeling the constantly increasing cold and depth of the snow ever more keenly, wondering whether they would ever find their way out of this precipitous, icy wilderness. Feed for the horses and mules ran out, and the animals became weak and frantic from hunger. Pawing the ground in search of grass that was not there, they would turn desperately in the direction from which they had come, trying to go back. With no other resource they began to eat their rawhide tethers, and the blankets that covered them at night. They gnawed at each other's manes and tails, which rapidly became ragged. The rigging of the pack saddles was gnawed until it became almost useless.

The cold was so bitter and the snow-laden gale raged with such force against the men that they could not see where they were going and, after a futile attempt to advance, returned to their camp to sit despondently near the bodies of several dead mules. The campfires melted deep holes in the snow, in which the men huddled miserably, choking and half blinded with the smoke of fires that did not warm them.

Some ten or twelve men, according to Frémont's later account to Jessie, had frozen faces, hands, or feet. "The guide became nigh frozen to death here," he wrote, "and dead mules were already lying about the fires. . . . Westward the country was buried in deep snow. It was impossible to advance, and to turn back was equally impracticable. We were overtaken by sudden and inevitable ruin."

It was a desperate situation calling for a desperate

A terrific snowstorm

remedy. Frémont decided that the only safe course open
to them lay in retreat. Along the Rio Grande they might
find game, and at the somewhat lower altitude the cold
would be less intense. The few pack animals that still
lived were so weak from starvation and cold as to be
useless. Frémont wrote to Jessie:

It was apparent that we should lose every animal. . . .
With great labor the baggage was transported across the
crest to the head springs of a little stream leading to the
main river. A few days were sufficient to destroy our fine
band of mules. They generally kept huddled together, and
as they froze, one would be seen to tumble down and the
snow would cover him; sometimes they would break off
and run toward the timber until they were stopped by the
deep snow, where they were soon hidden. . . .

It took the party more than a week to move the camp
and the baggage a distance of two miles. Christmas Day
was spent in deep dejection; Christmas dinner was mule
meat—all that was left to eat. The frozen carcasses of
mules that had died were eaten first, and then those that
were left, all of them too weak to be of any service,
were killed and eaten, for there was no game stirring in
this frozen wilderness.

Desperate now, Frémont called for volunteers to go
to one of the Spanish settlements of New Mexico to
obtain provisions and fresh mules or horses to take the
party to Taos. From among them he chose King, Brack-

enridge, Creutzfeldt, and the guide, Bill Williams. Shortly after this group left the camp, the first death occurred among the remaining men. A man named Proue simply spread his blankets on the snow, lay on them, and froze to death.

A bitter disappointment met them when they reached the Rio Grande, where they expected to find game. The deep snow had driven every living thing into shelter elsewhere. The expedition had little more than two weeks' supply of food and no prospect of replenishing it!

When sixteen days had passed and there was no sign of the relief expedition, Frémont started off himself with four picked men, including Godey and Preuss, carrying scant provisions for two or three days only. On the evening of the sixth day after leaving camp, the twenty-second since the relief party had left, Frémont and his men came upon Creutzfeldt, Brackenridge, and Williams huddled together. "The most miserable objects I have ever seen," Frémont wrote to Jessie. "I did not recognize Creutzfeldt's features when Brackenridge brought him up to me and mentioned his name. They had been starving. King had starved to death a few days before."

On the day before his meeting with the three survivors, Frémont had met a Utah Indian, son of a chief with whom he had been friendly. He gave the young man a rifle and two of his blankets and persuaded him to go along and act as guide, and to bring with him four horses. "Wretchedly poor," Frémont called the mounts, but they proved useful in getting Creutzfeldt, Brackenridge, and Williams—all of whom were too weak to walk —to Red River Settlement on the tenth evening after Frémont left the camp at the Rio Grande. During this time Frémont and his companions had walked 160 miles through deep snow. "I looked upon the anxiety which induced me to set out from camp as an inspiration," he wrote Jessie. "Had I remained there waiting the party which had been sent in, every man of us would probably have perished."

The day after reaching the Red River Settlement Godey and Frémont set out for Taos. Here about thirty animals were quickly collected, and these, along with a fresh stock of provisions and four Mexicans in charge of Godey were sent back to the encampment on the Rio Grande. Frémont stayed on for a time as the guest of Kit Carson, making plans to continue his expedition by a somewhat more southerly route.

The terrible story of what had happened to the men left in the Rio Grande camp was told by Frémont in a later addition to his letter to Jessie:

Including Mr. King and Proue we have lost eleven of our party. . . . You will remember that I left the camp with occupation sufficient to employ them for three or four days, after which they were to follow me down the river. Within that time I had expected relief from King, . . .

They remained where I had left them seven days, and then started down the river. Manuel—you will remember Manuel, The Cosumne Indian—gave way to a feeling of

despair after they had travelled about two miles, begged
Haler to shoot him, and then made his way back to camp;
intending to die there, as he doubtless soon did. They followed our trail down the river—twenty-two men they were
in all. About ten miles below the camp Wise gave out, threw
away his gun and blanket, and a few hundred yards further
fell over in the snow and died. Two Indian boys, young
men, countrymen of Manuel, were behind. They rolled up
Wise in his blanket and buried him in the snow on the river
bank. . . . Carver raved during the night, his imagination
wholly occupied with images of many things which he
fancied himself eating. In the morning he wandered off from
the party and probably soon died. They did not see him
again. Sorel on this day gave out and lay down to die. They
built him a fire, and Morin, who was in a dying condition,
and snow-blind, remained. These two did not probably last
till the next morning. That evening, I think Hubbard killed a
deer. They travelled on, getting here and there a grouse, but
probably nothing else, the snow having frightened off the
game.

The tragic story went on, telling how Haler, fearing
that the starving men would resort to cannibalism, suggested that the party break up into several small groups,
which it did. Haler went on with five other white men
and two Indian boys. The three Kern brothers and five
other men made a second party. Two of the men decided
to encamp where they were and wait for the relief party.
The deaths continued until Godey's party reached the
foremost of the several groups and rescued those alive.

Though Frémont had written Jessie that eleven men had died, he wrote later to Senator Benton giving the number as ten. In either case it was a staggering tragedy. Frémont's despondency is reflected in the longing to be with Jessie expressed at the end of the letter telling her of the sad events.

When I think of you all, I feel a warm glow at my heart, which renovates it like a good medicine, and I forget painful feelings in strong hope for the future. We shall yet, dearest wife, enjoy quiet and happiness together—these are nearly one and the same thing to me now. I make frequently pleasant pictures of the happy home we are to have, and oftenest and among the pleasantest of all I see our library with its bright fire in the rainy stormy days, and the large windows looking out upon the sea in the bright weather.

Who was to blame for the tragic outcome of the expedition? Some censured Frémont. Others said that the fault lay with Bill Williams who had chosen the wrong pass over the mountains. Frémont, although torn by sadness at the loss of so many good men, nevertheless immediately laid plans for continuing the expedition by a different route. Regardless of tragedy he would do what he had set out to do.

Gold for the Senator
from California

✠

*O*N AN ADDITION to his letter to Jessie, written February 6, 1849, Frémont told of his plans for continuing the expedition along a somewhat different route from that on which the tragic interruption of the journey occurred.

Tomorrow a friend sets out to purchase me a few mules with which he is to meet me at Albuquerque, and thence I continue my journey on my own animals. My road will take me down the Del Norte [the Rio Grande] about 160 miles below Albuquerque and then passes between this river and the heads of the Gila, to a little Mexican town called, I think, Tusson [Tucson]. Thence to the mouth of the Gila and across the Colorado, direct to Agua Caliente, into California. I intend to make the journey rapidly, and about the middle of March hope for the great pleasure of hearing from home.

Frémont had received invaluable assistance from Major Edward F. Beale, who had been associated with him on the third expedition, and who was now commanding army forces in northern New Mexico. Beale lent him horses and sold him provisions from the commissary. Others came to his aid also—Kit Carson, Dick Owens, Lucien Maxwell, and Francis Aubrey were among them. Aubrey lent him $1,000.

Several of the survivors of the retreat from the Rockies volunteered to go with him. Among them, to Frémont's delight, were Godey and McGehee. The three Kern brothers, Bill Williams, and a few others, declined. He hired others to replace them. When the expedition set out once more it consisted of twenty-five men, including a Mexican guide, and sixty horses. Frémont's notes of the expedition show that the route he actually took coincided most of the way with the one he had planned and outlined in his letter to Jessie.

He was eager to get to San Francisco as quickly as possible, not only to be there to welcome Jessie when she arrived, but also to try to settle an "error" that looked suspiciously as though it might be something else. When he had given Thomas Larkin $3,000 with which to buy him a ranch, he had definitely specified a tract near San Francisco with good farming land and an excellent view over the bay. Larkin instead had bought for him a tract of wild land in the foothills of the Sierras, in central California, over a hundred miles from the ocean and far removed from any settlement. The Mariposas, or Mariposa tract, as it was called, were seventy square miles in area, over 43,000 acres. But it was a region in which hostile Indians were numerous, and grazing cattle on it would have merely invited Indian cattle thieves. Frémont was furious.

However, as he followed the south bank of the Gila River, with Tucson behind him, something happened that made him less angry. There was a tremendous cloud of dust ahead of him. When it was blown aside for a moment, he saw figures of men, animals, and wagons. He hurried ahead and caught up with the rear guard. But still he could not see the head of the column, which Jessie later estimated, from her husband's account, as 1,200 men, women, and bawling babies and children. Never, in the days when the Oregon Trail had been crowded with emigrants, had he seen such a horde at one time.

"Where are you all going?" he asked.

"Alta California."

"But why so many of you?"

"Gold! Gold!"

This was the beginning of what has come to be known as the Gold Rush of '49. These were an advance host of the "Forty-niners." It was the first news Frémont had heard of the discovery of gold on Sutter's ranch, and the beginning, incidentally, of Sutter's loss of his vast holdings. Slowing his horse, to drop back and escape some of the dust, Frémont became thoughtful. Perhaps the Mariposa tract was not so bad after all. Seventy square miles! Nearly 45,000 acres! If Sutter's ranch was underlaid with gold, why not the Mariposa tract?

Always impetuous, Frémont at once arranged with twenty-eight Mexicans to work his land as a gold-yielding tract. He would grubstake them, and the gold that they found was to be divided equally.

Meanwhile Jessie had been suffering hardship on her journey to California. Crossing the Isthmus she had been poled up the Chagres River in a slow boat, beset by heat, flies, and mosquitoes, and had finished the trip by mule train, sleeping in camps of surveyors for a railway. At Panama she met a group of "Forty-niners" who told her the tragic story of her husband's expedition. Here she found that there was no boat leaving for California. The one she had expected to sail on had been deserted at San Francisco by all of its crew, for all had joined the gold rush. The hotel at Panama was indescribably bad, but luckily Jessie had letters of introduction to residents of Panama and was able to stay at the home of Madame Arcé, where she collapsed with fever.

As she was convalescing, two ships arrived: the *Panama* from around Cape Horn; and the *California*, which had managed to get a makeshift crew at San Francisco and had made the return trip. Jessie sailed on the *Panama*. Rumors had reached her that her husband had lost a leg in the debacle of the expedition, and she hoped desperately that there would be news at San Diego. But, according to her daughter, Lilly, when the boat arrived there, she locked herself in her stateroom, rather than face the news that might greet her, fearing that it might be unbearable. However, the ship had been docked only a few minutes when a man knocked at her door and shouted, "The colonel's safe; riding up to San Francisco to meet you; he didn't lose a leg—was only badly frostbitten."

For all Frémont's eagerness and the slowness of sea

transportation in 1849, Jessie reached San Francisco before her husband. She found a town gone mad with gold fever—practically deserted by its permanent inhabitants, and crowded to overflowing with newcomers on their way to a gold field they could exploit. The transients lived in whatever sort of shelter they could find or put together: ragged tents, sheds made of scraps of lumber, shelters made of blankets—anything that would give them even a little protection from the elements.

By a piece of luck Jessie managed to rent a furnished adobe house in which to live until her husband arrived. And there she stayed, trying to avoid the hurlyburly of the town about her, with its sudden wealth that attracted gamblers and confidence men, and the disheartening spectacle of those who came back impoverished from diggings that yielded nothing.

At last Frémont arrived, and for a time their joy at being together was enough to keep them from making any future plans. But the climate of San Francisco did not agree with Jessie, and besides it was too far from the Mariposa ranch. So they decided to go to Monterey where they would still be more than a hundred miles from the estate, but at least would be nearer than they were in San Francisco.

At Monterey, they were hospitably offered a wing in the house of the former governor Castro, whose wife still lived in another wing, though Castro himself was in Mexico. Though he kept Monterey as his headquarters, Frémont spent much time at the ranch, riding the hundred and forty miles to it on horseback, or sometimes,

President Zachary Taylor

with Jessie, in a six-seater surrey, the cushions of which made an excellent mattress on which to sleep at night while on the road. Frémont built a frame house on the ranch, a vast expanse of natural beauty with pine trees two hundred feet high, as thick as the height of a man, and tumbling streams filled with fish, and with gold.

It was while he was happily engaged in overseeing the immensely productive gold-panning operations on his ranch that Frémont received gratifying news from Washington. Zachary Taylor, who had commanded United States troops in the Mexican War, had become President of the United States on March 5, 1849. Neigh-

borly relations with Mexico made it necessary to determine exactly where the boundary line between the two
countries was, and Taylor appointed Frémont to direct
a survey. Frémont's attitude toward the appointment
was expressed later in a letter to Jacob R. Snyder of San
Francisco:

I regarded the commission as a disavowal on the part
of the President of the proceedings recently held against
me. Respect to the President, together with a full appreciation of the consideration which had induced him to make
the appointment, did not, in my judgment, permit me to
decline, and I accordingly accepted the commission, with
the intention which I then expressed to Mr. Beale and others
shortly to resign.

And resign he did, for both business and political
affairs were filling every moment of his life.

Fortunately, the men Frémont had hired to work the
gold on his land had proved to be honest, and according
to Jessie, her husband's share was sent to Monterey in
buckskin sacks, each of which contained some $25,000
worth of gold.

But their good fortune turned out to be a mixed
blessing. As soon as the news got about that such quantities of gold were being washed out of the gravel of the
Mariposa streams, others rushed to the region, and soon
they were swarming over Frémont's land. Under the
Mexican law, which had not been replaced by American

law, the transfer of land did not include mineral rights, and Frémont was powerless to stop the horde of what today would be called trespassers. But at first it mattered little, because there seemed to be enough for all.

The man who was both explorer and enterpriser was also busy now with politics.

By the end of 1849 the population of California had swollen to over a hundred thousand. A convention of delegates at Monterey had adopted a constitution which forbade slavery, and had applied for admission as a state to the union. Throughout all of the proceedings, and even before the convention had met, Frémont had been talked of as a candidate for the senatorship. A Democrat, he belonged to the Free Soil branch of that party. No other single man had had so much to do with the settlement of California as he; none saw its problems more clearly than he did. He strongly urged the building of a cross-continental railroad which would connect California with the East, and had shown, in his last expedition, by what route it might be laid. He would, it was clear, do all in his power, if elected, to bring such a railroad into being. He was unalterably opposed to slavery, and anti-slavery forces were in the ascendancy in California at the time. So it surprised no one when, in December 1849, he was elected, along with William M. Gwynn, to what, in fact, would not be an office until California became a state nine months later.

On the night of January 1, 1850, the Frémonts left San Francisco by ship for the East, via the Panama route. On the trip across the Isthmus both Jessie and her husband became ill with Chagres fever (a malignant type of malaria) from the effects of which they were still suffering when they finally reached Washington. Because of this Frémont was unable to accept another honor that was offered him—an invitation to attend, as an advisor, a convention at Philadelphia for the purpose of promoting a national road to the Pacific Ocean. He did, however, write the members of the committee at great length, reporting on his fourth expedition, and demonstrating the practicality of the project.

On September 9, 1850, California was admitted as the thirty-first state of the union, and the following day Frémont took his seat as one of her senators. There was some opposition to his being seated, on technical grounds. Jefferson Davis, then a senator from Mississippi, later to be President of the Confederate States of America, moved that Frémont's credentials be referred to a committee for examination before he was seated. The motion was overruled, however, and Frémont immediately went into action.

Between his seating on September 9, 1850, and the expiration of his term on the third of March 1851, the Senate sat for only three weeks. However, during that brief time, the new senator introduced eighteen bills—all concerning the welfare of the state that had sent him to Washington: a bill to provide for the recording of California land titles, a bill to provide for the survey of public lands in California, two bills designed to aid in public education, and others.

Fire, and Retreat to Europe

✠

ACK IN CALIFORNIA, after his brief and active career as a senator, Frémont devoted himself to the affairs of the Mariposa ranch, and a campaign for re-election to the Senate. The population of California in 1850 had grown to 122,000, and the pro-slavery wing of the Democratic Party had increased in strength. Slave labor was wanted by many to gather the golden harvest resulting from the panning of gravel and the digging of ore, and Frémont had expressed so strongly his conviction that slavery was evil that he was defeated.

The defeat was undoubtedly a disappointment to him, but he had little time to think about it, for the Mariposa Ranch affairs, much more complicated than a campaign for re-election, kept him busy. His difficulties there were legion. The boundaries of the ranch had never been clearly established. The question of his title was clouded by differences between Mexican law (under which he had acquired his claim) and American, under which he actually had no title, for the Congress had refused to confirm title to any California lands without written proof of ownership. This Frémont could not get, for the records of the Mexican administration were under lock and key in various repositories, and no one seemed to know what papers were where. Claim jumpers swarmed over his land, many of them defending their own claims with shotguns. What had seemed a treasure trove was rapidly becoming a large problem with no immediate hope of a solution.

In the early summer of 1850 Frémont began, through an agent in London, to sell mining leases to British mining companies. Some sales were made apparently, but when the British purchasers learned of the legal tangle in which the claim was involved, there were loud complaints and, in the fall of 1851, Frémont ordered that no more sales were to be made until the matter of his own claim was cleared up.

During 1851 he launched a new business enterprise—supplying beef to Indians. Miners, thronging the foothills of the mountains and valleys, had driven the Indians away from their hunting grounds, and they had become troublesome. To replace the wild game they had previously found on these hunting grounds, their hunger forced them to kill cattle that belonged to settlers. In return, the settlers attacked the Indians, and a general war seemed imminent. Washington, alarmed, sent commissioners to discuss the matter with the Indian leaders, and it was decided that the only successful solution to the problem would be to furnish beef to the hungry redskins. Frémont's bid was the lowest rendered by a responsible bidder, and he furnished, from cattle fed on his ranch, some $180,000 worth of meat—and then found

Jessie Benton Frémont
in middle age

that there was no government appropriation from which his bill could be paid.

During the time when he was active at the ranch, Jessie spent most of her time at the Frémont's hillside house on Stockton Street in San Francisco. Here, on April 19, 1851, her third child, and second son, was born, and named John Charles Frémont—the third in line to bear the name. Fifteen days later, on May 4, while she was still bedridden, fire roared through much of the city, the flames and smoke surging past Jessie's window and lighting the night with a lurid glow. Articles of especial value were quickly removed from the house and taken to that of a friend who lived out of the path of the blaze; carpets soaked in water were hung on the walls of the house against the heat; and preparations were made to move Jessie at once if it became necessary. But the fire-fighters, working frantically throughout the night, stopped the advance of the flaming terror before it reached the Frémont house.

A second fire, however, which occurred late in June, advanced so rapidly that it soon became evident that the house on Stockton Street could not be saved. Frémont was at the ranch, and Jessie had to decide what was best herself. Unable to salvage any of the contents of the house, she and her baby went to the home of a friend higher on the hillside. Here she sat at a window and watched while her house burned to the ground. She now moved into a dwelling that was bare of all conveniences. But this condition, more like camping out than living in a home, did not last long, because of an act of almost unbelievable kindness.

Frémont had invested in a fairly large tract of land in San Francisco, and had leased it to a group of English immigrants, who had built on it a brewery and a number of cottages. A delegation of these tenants came to the house in which Jessie was staying, some carrying parcels, some drawing loaded carts. Their leader explained quietly that when they saw the fire advancing toward the Frémont home, a group of them had gone to see what they could do to help. Finding Jessie gone, they had joined forces, and, working against time as the destroying flames advanced, had taken out of the house everything of value that they could, which was, in fact, almost everything in it. They now brought the Frémont furniture, mirrors, china and glass, hundreds of books, even kitchen utensils, and all of the clothing they found in the house. One of the women apologized for having laundered some soiled clothing, saying, "I thought you might be so put about with the changing, the clothes would have long to wait." Then the crowning kindness came, when one of the men put on the table a heavy parcel tied in a red silk handkerchief. "We knew the master was from home," he said, "and there was a young babbie in the house, and we thought money might come in handy, so we brought a quarter's rent in advance."

At this point, as she herself reported the incident, Jessie wept, so moved that she was able in no other way to express her gratitude.

Nor was Frémont ungrateful when, filled with anxiety, he hurried home to find only a single chimney, a stark, fire-blackened column, to mark where his house had stood, but Jessie safe and the baby safe, surrounded by all of the familiar household objects. His English tenants had frequently told him that they would like to buy their home sites, but he had always refused. Now he hurried to thank them, and told them that, as a token of his gratitude to them, he was having deeds to all of the lots prepared, at a nominal price.

Aside from the fact that San Francisco was a sorry sight that summer of 1851, two other considerations impelled the Frémonts to leave it temporarily. One was Jessie's health, which had been affected by the shocks of the two fires while she was still weak from childbirth; the other was Frémont's need of capital for developing the Mariposa property. He thought England was the only place in which he could get this money. They traveled east by the Panama route and sailed from New York for Liverpool in the spring of 1852 in the old Cunard Line sidewheel steamer *Africa.*

In London, rooms had been reserved for them at the Clarendon Hotel by the Marchioness of Wellesley who, as Miss Caton of Maryland, had long been a friend of Jessie's. Abbot Lawrence, United States Minister to the Court of St. James, and his wife, arranged a program of entertainment so strenuous that it made even the excitement-loving Jessie wince a little. Later she wrote with the joyousness of happy memories of many dinners and teas in London high society, and of her presentation to Queen Victoria, who gave her, she reported, "an impression of womanly goodness combined with a look of power." They met the Duke of Wellington, who greeted them cordially, his sparkling eyes seeming to belie his age and failing strength. They also met Roderick Murchison, president of the Royal Geographical Society, who questioned Frémont in detail about his western explorations.

From London they went to Paris where, having met the Comte de la Garde, they were introduced to Paris society, where their welcome bespoke the high regard the French had for the Pathfinder.

The Frémonts saw Louis Napoleon's installation as Emperor, and were given a special place on the official tribune, from which they watched the colorful parade celebrating the return of the imperial eagles to the French standards. They went to many fêtes, balls, and court affairs, including a *dansant* given by Louis Napoleon himself.

By invitation, Frémont and Jessie attended the colorful ceremony celebrating the Emperor's marriage to the

Spanish Eugénie Maria de Montijo Ouyman of Granada, daughter of the Conte de Teba and a Scottish noble-woman. After the ceremony they watched the glittering wedding procession, which included the famous gold-crowned glass coach in which Marie Antoinette and the royal Marie Louise had once ridden. Within it, on a seat covered with white satin, rode the Emperor, his uniform gay with stars and decorations, and his pale, unsmiling bride, wearing a wedding dress of white velvet and a veil made by the lacemakers of Alençon.

In Paris, on February 1, 1853, the Frémonts' fourth child was born, named Anne Beverly after Frémont's mother. She died six months later at the home of Jessie's relative Francis Preston Blair, at Silver Springs, Maryland, near Washington.

In the meantime, title to the Mariposa ranch had not yet been established; the claim on the national treasury for $180,000 for the beef supplied to the Indians had not been paid; nor had the government yet acknowledged responsibility for debts Frémont had incurred as commander of the California Battalion, and claims against him were becoming troublesome. A lawsuit for $19,500, brought by a man named Huttman, was now pending. (Eventually the Congress paid the interest on this debt and the costs of a judgment against Frémont, all of which amounted to $48,814. Strangely there seems to be no record of the principal amount ever having been paid.) It was time for Frémont to get home and take charge.

And there was another compelling reason for his

return. The United States government had, early in 1852, taken an active interest in a transcontinental railway project, and had ordered five different routes to be explored in order to select the best. Jefferson Davis, then Secretary of War, who had opposed Frémont's being seated in the Senate, chose the routes and appointed five different groups of men, all headed by army officers, to carry out the explorations and surveys. Frémont was not among those chosen to lead one of the exploring expeditions, and he was, quite understandably, offended.

He decided that he would make his own exploration, paying for it out of his own funds. On his arrival in California in 1849, after the misadventure of his fourth expedition, he had announced that, in spite of the tragedy, the expedition had accomplished its purpose. Nevertheless, he was not satisfied with the results of it. He planned to go back to the spot where he had let Bill Williams choose the route, and take the route that he had preferred in an attempt to complete the exploration in the way he had originally intended.

That is why, about the middle of September 1853, Frémont was once more at Westport Landing on the Missouri, where his ill-fated fourth expedition had been launched. From here, also, he would launch his fifth, and last, expedition.

The Fifth, and Last, Expedition

☩

HE FIFTH EXPEDITION, as it left Westport Landing, consisted of twenty-two men, of
whom ten were Delaware Indians. Preuss would have
been one of the men, but his wife, remembering the
fourth expedition, persuaded him not to go. In his place
Frémont engaged S. N. Carvallo of Baltimore, who
brought with him a bulky outfit for taking daguerreotype
pictures. According to Carvallo's report, the expedition
had provisions to sustain seventy men for a month.

After three days of traveling, Frémont became ill.
He returned to Westport Landing for medical advice,
instructing his party to meet him at a place three days'
journey from where they now were. But from Westport
he sent a messenger saying that he had to return to St.
Louis, and that the expedition was to proceed to a place
known as "Smoky Hills," on a fork of the Kansas River,
where plenty of buffalo would be found. From there
they were to send back Chief Solomon, one of the Delawares, who would meet their leader at Westport and
conduct him to the camp in about two weeks.

Thirty days later, they were still encamped on the

Kansas River waiting for Frémont, and were concerned for his safety. Suddenly there was further cause for alarm. They saw a cloud of smoke to the east so dense that it almost obscured the sun. A vast expanse of prairie between their camp and Westport Landing was burning! At night the sky was lit with a reddish glow that brightened as the flaming line advanced toward them. The belt of fire extended as far as the eye could see. Their encampment had the Kansas River on one side, Solomon's Fork on another, Salt Creek on the third, and a large belt of woods on the fourth, so the men were fairly secure from danger, but they knew that Frémont would have to ride through the fire in order to reach them. They dared not move. For one thing, there was no place to which they could go where they would be so well protected and, for another, this was the place Chief Solomon would expect to find them. Frémont's dramatic return was described by Carvallo in a slim book that he wrote about the expedition.

Just after breakfast one of the Delawares gave a loud whoop and pointed to the burning prairie before us, where, to our great joy, we saw Colonel Frémont, followed by an immense man, who proved to be the doctor, on an immense mule, and the Indian chief and his servant, galloping through the blazing element in the direction of our camp. Instantly with one accord all the men discharged their rifles in a volley, our tents were struck, and we wanted to make a signal for their guidance. We all reloaded, and when they

"We saw Colonel Frémont . . . galloping through the blazing element in the direction of our camp"

were very near, we fired a salute. Our men and Indians instantly surrounded Colonel Frémont with kind inquiries after his health. No father who had been absent from his children could have been received with more enthusiasm and real joy. To reach us he had to travel over nearly fifty miles of country which had been on fire. . . .

The route of the expedition was, in general, that of the previous one, except that they avoided the Carnero

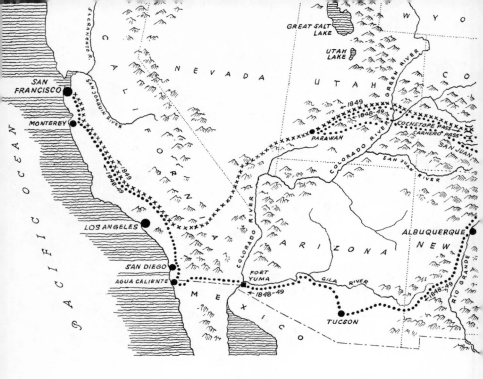

Pass over the San Juan Range, southwest of Pueblo, where they had faced disaster in the mountains, and took an alternate way through the Cochetope Pass, where they found the snow light and easily negotiated, thus confirming Frémont's opinion that a railroad was completely practical. Yet even so there were times when it seemed as though the disaster of the fourth expedition was to be repeated. Provisions, which had been depleted during the month-long wait for Frémont, gave out and, according to Carvallo's account, they were forced to slaughter horses one at a time for food. At one point the conditions seemed so grave that Frémont administered an oath to all the men by which they bound themselves, no matter how desperate they became for food, not to

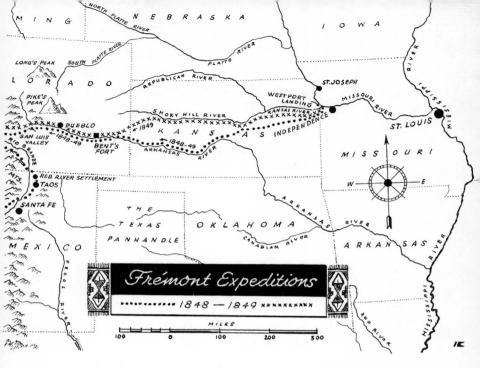

resort to cannibalism. One of the men, Oliver Fuller of
St. Louis, froze his feet badly and, on the day before the
party reached the Mormon settlement of Parawan, where
all could be made comfortable, Fuller died, sitting on his
horse, where he was held by two of his companions, one
walking on each side of him. "He died like a man, on
horseback in his saddle," Frémont wrote Senator Benton,
"and will be buried like a soldier . . . where he fell."

Though the exact route that Frémont's party followed on the fifth expedition was never used for a railroad, Frémont's report was helpful in proving that the
transcontinental road was practical, and that the general
route he had followed was about a hundred miles shorter
than any that had been followed before.

In May 1854, Frémont reached San Francisco, where he declined a public dinner planned in his honor because he wanted to get back to the East Coast as quickly as possible. One reason for this was his knowledge that the fifth Frémont child was due. Frank Preston Frémont was born on May 17, 1854, before Frémont reached Washington.

After his return, he wrote a long report on the results of his expedition which was published in the *Washington National Intelligencer* on June 13, 1854. He spent some time in New York, working in the studio of the photographer Mathew Brady, who was to become famous for his Civil War pictures. Here Frémont helped to finish the daguerreotypes taken by Carvallo on the expedition. And here he received the good news that his claim against the government for the beef he had supplied to the Indians had at last been approved. One of his anxieties was now removed.

The larger one, however—clearing up his claim to the Mariposa ranch—still remained, a dark cloud in his sky.

Frémont for President

✠

N THE SPRING of 1855, the Frémont family
moved to New York. Washington had become a
city of sad memories for Jessie who had, within a short
time, suffered the death of her mother and the shock of
seeing the Benton mansion burn to the ground. Jessie
spent much of that summer of 1855 at Siasconset on
Nantucket while Frémont divided his time between New
York and Washington, keeping busy with the affairs of
the Mariposa ranch. That year the Supreme Court at last
confirmed his claim to the estate. He was about to leave
for California to go to the ranch, when word reached
him that leaders of the Democratic Party, of which he
was a member, were considering nominating him for the
Presidency of the United States.

Support for the nomination was offered to him at a
hotel in New York by influential leaders. But there were
certain conditions. In order to gain their support (which
would almost undoubtedly bring about his nomination)
he would have had to agree to endorse the Kansas-
Nebraska Act and the Fugitive Slave Law. He knew that
his endorsement of either of these laws would be inter-

preted as an endorsement of slavery, and he had made it quite clear that he was irrevocably opposed to that institution.

There is no question, however, that he was tempted. The Democrats were his party and their leaders were offering him a chance to obtain the highest honor that America could give to one of its sons. He asked for a little time to consider, and went to Siasconset to talk it over with his wife.

Jessie later told how they walked together to Lighthouse Hill, where her husband told her of the offer.

At the foot of the bluff on which the lighthouse stood, were the remains embedded in the sands of a ship, the seas washing into her ribs. Above, steady and brilliant, flashed out the recurring light. "It is the choice between a wreck of dishonor or a kindly light that will go on its mission of doing good. You cannot give in . . ." And so his decision was made.

But if his own party, the Democrats, would not have him on his own terms, there was another group of men, in the process of becoming a national party, who would. These were leaders of the new Republican, or "People's," party, which existed as a rapidly growing group of state parties. In February 1856, Republican delegates from nine states met at Philadelphia to form a national party based solidly on the declaration that slavery must not be extended into states in which it did not already exist, and that laws permitting slavery in territories that had been free must be repealed.

At the end of the national party meeting at Philadelphia, possible candidates for President were being discussed by the leaders. Among them were Salmon Portland Chase, William H. Seward (later to be Lincoln's Secretary of State), and Frémont, who had declined the offer of nomination by his own party. Later, in April, Frémont reiterated his position on slavery:

I am opposed to slavery in the abstract and upon principle, sustained and made habitual by long settled convictions. While I feel inflexible in the belief that it ought not to be interfered with where it exists, under the shield of State sovereignty, I am as inflexibly opposed to its extension on this continent beyond its present limits.

Among those favored for the vice-presidential nomination were Abraham Lincoln, then an Illinois lawyer, and W. L. Dayton.

Nathaniel P. Banks of Massachusetts, also a Democrat but, like Frémont, an ardent Free Soiler who had broken with his party over the question of extending slavery, supported Frémont, though he himself was also discussed as a possible presidential candidate. It was Banks who interested John Bigelow in the Frémont candidacy. Bigelow was assistant to William Cullen Bryant, the poet, who was at the time editor of the *Evening Post* in New York. After an interview with Frémont, Bigelow became one of his campaign managers and called a conference of Free Soil leaders, among whom were Francis P. Blair, Samuel J. Tilden, Edwin D. Morgan (former member of the New York State Senate, and later Governor of New York), all of whom agreed to support the Pathfinder.

The early Republicans worked rapidly! Immediately Bryant's *Evening Post* expressed its support of Frémont. Other papers—especially in the Middle West and West—followed the *Evening Post's* example. The campaign was furthered by four hastily written biographies, three for adults and one for young people, all praising Frémont as the "Champion of Freedom" and "Columbus of the Golden West." One of these had a sale of thirty thousand copies—a large sale for a book today and a tremendous one for 1856, when the population of the United States was about thirty million—less than one-sixth that of to-day. The most impressive of the four books was written by John Bigelow and Jessie Frémont, though it bears only Bigelow's name. It remains today one of the best sources for a biography of Frémont, lavishly supplied with letters and other documents.

On June 17, the first Republican national nominating convention met in the Musical Fund Hall of Philadelphia. From the start, Frémont's name was foremost. On the third day he was nominated. W. L. Dayton was named as vice-presidential candidate.

As the campaign gathered momentum, there were two other party tickets of importance: Buchanan and Breckinridge were the choice of the Democrats; Fillmore and Donelson were the candidates of the Whig Party. They were to be the last candidates of this party, which had almost died in its defeat in 1852, and now was actually dying.

Support for the Republican candidate spread rapidly. Longfellow gave up a trip to Europe in order to speak and vote for him. Washington Irving, Ralph Waldo Emerson, John Greenleaf Whittier, William Cullen Bryant, Horace Greeley (founder and editor of the New York *Tribune*, who, in his paper, called the followers of Buchanan "the Buchaneers"), Henry Ward Beecher, and other anti-slavery advocates of note campaigned for the Pathfinder, in whom they found their ideal candidate. "Rocky Mountain" clubs, "Frémont and Freedom" clubs, and, in California, dozens of "Bear" clubs were formed to support him.

Torchlight parades throughout the country carried banners bearing such slogans as "We'll take the Buck [Buchanan] by the Horns," "Free Labor, Free Speech, Free Men, Free Kansas, and Frémont," etc. There were tremendous mass demonstrations in support of him—in which 25,000 participated at Massilon, Ohio; 30,000 at Kalamazoo; about the same number at Beloit, Wisconsin. Lincoln spoke for Frémont to 10,000 people at Princeton and, according to one estimate, 35,000 at Alton, Illinois. At Jacksonville, a Frémont parade was a mile and a quarter long. At an Indianapolis demonstration, fifty bands are said to have participated. Young people banded together, calling themselves "Wide-awakes," and organized demonstrations. Such slogans as "We are a Buck-Hunting" and "Jessie Bent-on Being Free" appeared widely. Songs and poems praising Fré-

THE GREAT AMERICAN BUCK HUNT OF 1856.

*Newspaper cartoons that appeared during Frémont's campaign
for the Presidency*

COL FREMONT'S LAST GRAND EXPLORING EXPEDITION IN 1856.

mont and deriding his principal opponent, Buchanan, appeared.

Several poems were written by John Greenleaf Whittier. Parts of two follow:

> *Sound now the trumpet warningly!*
> *The storm is rolling nearer,*
> *The hour is striking clearer,*
> *In the dusky dome of sky.*
> *If dark and cold the morning be*
> *A darker morn before us*
> *Shall fling its shadow o'er us*
> *If we let the hour go by.*
> *Sound we then the trumpet chorus!*
> *Sound the onset wild and high!*
> *Country and Liberty!*
> *Freedom and Victory!*
> *These words shall be our cry—*
> *Frémont and Victory!*

In the second the "robber" stalking over "the prairie" personified the Democratic Party which refused to endorse the demand of Frémont and the Republicans that all new states admitted to the Union should be states in which slavery would be prohibited.

> *The robber o'er the prairie stalks,*
> *And calls the land his own,*
> *And he who talks as Slavery talks*
> *Is free to talk alone.*
> *But tell the knaves we are not slaves*

And tell them slaves we ne'er will be;
Come weal or woe, the world shall know
We're free, we're free, we're free!

One poem written by Whittier's sister, Elizabeth
Hussey Whittier, had a swinging lilt that made it as
memorable as a catchy melody:

As his mountain men follow, undoubting
    and bold,
O'er hill and o'er desert through tempest
    and cold,
And answer with shouting the wild bugle call,
Who'll follow? Who'll follow?
    The bands gather fast;
    They who ride with Frémont
    Ride in triumph at last.

Oh, speed the bold riders! Fling loose every
    rein,
The race run for freedom is not run in vain;
From mountain and prairie, from lake and
    from sea,
Ride gallant and hopeful, ride fearless and
    free!
Who'll follow? Who'll follow? Etc.

The shades of the fathers for freedom who
    died
As they rode in the war-storm now ride at
    our side;

*Their great souls shall strengthen our own
  for the fray,
And the glance of our leader make certain
  the way.
Then follow, then follow, Etc.*

*We ride not for honors, ambition, or place,
But the wrong to redress, and redeem the
  disgrace;
Not for North, nor for South, but the best
  good for all,
We follow Frémont, and his wild bugle call. Etc.*

The last two were originally printed in a magazine called *The Era,* on August 14, 1856, and set to music. Whittier's was unsigned; his sister's was signed simply "E." A letter from Whittier to a friend acknowledged the authorship of the first and credited the second to his sister, and they were reprinted under the two names in *The Independent* magazine on December 21, 1899.

But the opposition was vociferous, had much greater financial support than the Republicans, and fought with no regard for fair play. Frémont was charged by the Democrats with being pro-slavery and the owner of seventy-five slaves, in spite of his several public declarations to the contrary, and his rejection of the nomination offered him by the Democrats because of that party's stand on slavery. The support that he received from German immigrants prompted the charge that he was the candidate of the Germans, and therefore of all for-

eigners, rather than that of native-born Americans. Fillmore, the Whig candidate, insisted that, if elected, Frémont would be a "sectional President," concerned with
the welfare of the North only, and that his election
would be followed immediately by secession of the
southern states. This prediction was repeated and em-
phasized by a number of southern papers.

Perhaps Frémont's greatest disappointment in the
campaign arose from this charge that he would represent
the North only, for it brought about opposition from one
upon whom he had counted for strong and influential
support—his father-in-law, Senator Benton, who charged
that the whole Republican movement was aggravating
hostility between the North and South, and denounced
any political party that chose to elect its officers from
one section only. The South, he said, would never submit
to such a President as Frémont.

Other charges were brought against the Republican
candidate. Though all of his friends knew that he was
one of the most abstemious of human beings, the charge
was made that he was a heavy drinker. It was stated
that he was actually ineligible to be President, since he
had been born abroad and was not really an American
citizen. The Los Angeles *Star* reported that he had
been cruel and greedy in his treatment of the Mexican-
Californians during and after the Bear Flag War. One
after another the false charges were built up against him.
Most of them Frémont decided not to dignify by an
answer.

And, false though they were, they undoubtedly damaged his candidacy greatly, and turned many against him whose support he had counted on. Among the most important of these was William Lloyd Garrison, the voluble abolitionist, who, saying that the Republican program was vague and ineffective, was active in selecting an "Abolitionist" ticket headed by Gerrit Smith.

This kind of opposition, the explosive character of the issue of slavery, on which Frémont refused to make any compromise, and a perhaps not unnatural distrust of a newly formed political party, were too much even for Frémont's tremendous popularity to overcome. When the election returns were all in it was found that, though Frémont had received 1,340,000 votes, Buchanan had carried nineteen of the thirty-one states, Frémont eleven, and Fillmore one.

Frémont took the defeat philosophically; he had long since learned—and the lesson had become deeply imbedded on his fourth expedition—how to meet setbacks. But the fourteen-year-old Lilly, who had built dream castles about living in the White House, broke down and wept inconsolably.

Four years later, in the second national election in which there was a Republican candidate, that candidate won. His name was Abraham Lincoln.

A Little War, and the
Beginning of a Great One

✠

WHEN THE ELECTION furor had sub-
sided, Frémont went to California with the
intention of developing the ranch. But the Supreme
Court's action, confirming his title, did not by any means
put an end to his difficulties. His original grant had given
him seventy square miles of land with considerable freedom of choice as to its exact location. Frémont had
asked the state to measure off the land in an irregular
strip along both sides of the Merced River. When the
authorities refused this request, he chose a compact tract
that included several claims being worked by others.

It would have been impossible to select so large a
tract of land in this location without offending some
squatters, because prospectors had swarmed all over the
area during the western gold rush. Frémont chose his
location as the law allowed, but undoubtedly with an
eye to the best mining rights he could get. Even so,
many thought that he was trying to deprive them of
their rights, and a great deal of ill feeling resulted.

In the spring of 1857, Jessie went to Paris for a rest,
taking the children, but she was called back by what

proved to be the final illness of her father, Senator Benton. After his death, the Frémonts made their home at the Mariposa Ranch. Two ore mills were now in operation, producing a revenue of two or three thousand dollars a week, and the former candidate for the Presidency was constantly busy visiting the mills, or going to and from San Francisco or Monterey on business connected with the enterprise.

The Frémont household now consisted of Frémont and Jessie, their daughter, Lilly, their two surviving sons, Frémont's eighteen-year-old niece Nina, and two young men—Charles Douglas Fox, an English boy who was visiting them, and the twenty-one-year-old John R. Howard, son of a man who had given a great deal of help to Frémont in his Presidential campaign. It was a pleasant household in which no one except Frémont had any suspicion of impending trouble.

The peace they all enjoyed was shattered early one morning. One of the workmen woke Frémont and Jessie by knocking on the window of their bedroom. He announced that a number of miners working for the Hornitas League (a group that had joined together to remedy what they felt was Frémont's trespass on their claims) had taken possession of one of the richest shafts on the estate. They had found a way to do this legally—or so they claimed. Only a short time before this a California judge had held that a somewhat vague statute justified anyone's entering and holding any "unoccupied" mine. The Hornitas men had simply bribed Frémont's night watchman at this shaft to leave it "unoccupied," and had walked in and fortified themselves. In a shaft very close to the one the Hornitas men had entered, six of Frémont's miners were working.

These men, loyal to Frémont, barricaded themselves, using rocks, machinery, and kegs of powder to form a shield, and stayed put, while the Hornitas men lay nearby, their rifles at the ready, trying to figure out a way to take these two mines, and a third nearby, without bloodshed. As soon as Frémont learned of the trespass, he got a force of twenty men together and stood guard to keep reinforcements from joining the invaders. So long as no one fired a shot, nothing further happened. But everyone there knew that once shooting began it would be difficult to prevent serious bloodshed.

Fortunately no one fired the first shot, and the situation was saved chiefly by the ingenuity and courage of the seventeen-year-old Douglas Fox, who rode for reinforcements on Lilly's horse, Ayah. In order to avoid the guards posted along the roads, he led his mount through the woods and up a mountainside until he reached a point at which he would be out of sight of the invaders. Then he rode the animal as hard as he could to Coultersville, from which others carried his message to Stockton. As soon as the governor received the news, he sent five hundred members of the militia to Mariposa, and the Hornitas people were ejected.

Now Frémont pushed the development of his mining and smelting project still harder. The Merced River was dammed at great expense to furnish water power for a mill, a large force of Chinese workmen was brought in, and a private railroad was built to carry the ore a distance of over three miles. With the increase in the number of workmen, a village grew on the ranch, with shops, a village baker, and a cook to prepare food for the unmarried men. Horace Greeley, who visited the estate at about this time, estimated that the two mills at Mariposa produced at least $250,000 worth of gold a year, at a cost of not more than $100,000.

During Frémont's frequent business trips to San Francisco he was engaged in a project that Jessie didn't know about until she visited the city in 1859. Then she discovered that her husband, as a surprise for her, had built a charming house on a piece of high land that extended into the bay. Jessie later wrote that once she had entered the house all desire to return East left her. She wished only to stay there and make a home in which she and her husband and children could live together without being separated. This, she felt, would be their home for the rest of their lives. Here they would live out their days in peace and happiness.

But two things neither of the Frémonts could foresee once more disrupted their plans. First, the Mariposa mining venture was not actually as prosperous as Greeley had thought; second, the rapidly growing tension between the northern and southern states was about to explode into the violence of the Civil War.

Toward the end of 1860, after the election of Abraham Lincoln, the first Republican President of the United States, Frémont received unofficial word that Lincoln was ready to give him any cabinet position he chose. But trouble at Mariposa made him feel that he could not neglect the ranch. Badly in need of money to carry on his operations, Frémont left for Paris in January 1861, to try to obtain capital by selling half of the estate. When he reached New York, he had a conference with President Lincoln, who still believed that war could be avoided. Frémont hoped that he was right, but feared that he was wrong.

While Frémont was in Paris, he learned that his fears had been justified, when he received the news that, on April 12, Fort Sumter had been fired upon by the South. He at once wrote to Washington offering to serve in the Army of the United States. The reply to his offer, telling him that he had been commissioned as a major general—one of the first four men for whom this rank was authorized by Congress—made him prepare to start for home at once.

Unhappy Commander

✠

*D*URING HIS EXPEDITIONS to the West, when he was sometimes three thousand miles and several weeks away from the nation's capital, Frémont had learned to act on his own initiative without waiting for authority from Washington. To have done otherwise would often have placed him and his men in extreme danger. Now he showed the same independence.

Before he left Paris, Frémont learned that Confederate agents were in Europe buying war supplies. He immediately decided to buy arms for the Federal troops, without any authority from Washington and without any assurance that he would not, himself, have to pay for them. He went to London to see Charles Francis Adams, United States Minister to the Court of St. James, who approved of Frémont's plan. Adams drew $75,000 of government money to pay for cannon and shells that the doughty Pathfinder had bought in England, and 10,000 rifles he had contracted for in France.

Frémont reached Boston June 27, and hurried to Washington to report to President Lincoln. He was made Commander of the newly created Western Department of the Army. His headquarters would be in St. Louis, where he had first met the man who was later to become his enemy, General Kearny, and where he was now to encounter a still more formidable troublemaker.

Jessie wrote, later:

Everything was changed. There was no life on the river; the many steamboats were laid up at their wharves, their fires out, the singing, cheery crews gone—they, empty, swinging idly with the current. As we drove through the deserted streets we saw only closed shutters to warehouses and business places; the wheels and the horses' hoofs echoed loud and harsh as when one drives through the silent streets late in the night. It was a hostile city and showed itself as such.

It was indeed hostile—at least more than half of it was, for the state of Missouri was divided within itself, and in St. Louis the majority did not conceal their sympathy with the Southern Confederacy. Recruiting for the Confederate Army was carried on openly in a building over which flew the Stars and Bars of the South. The Confederate flag also waved on houses in the best residential districts. The few Union officers stationed at the St. Louis arsenal wisely stayed indoors after dark in order to avoid the gangs who prowled through the city, some armed, shouting their support for Jefferson Davis and the rebels.

Whether Missouri would remain with the Union or secede had been a question from the day that the Confederacy was formed. A group headed by Governor Claiborne F. Jackson held that the state must secede and stand beside her southern neighbors. A larger group, including a former governor and several influential editors, believed that, though secession might be necessary eventually, so grave a step ought not to be taken until every avenue toward a peaceful settlement of the differences between the North and the South had been explored. But in spite of the fact that Missouri had not actually seceded, Governor Jackson had called fifty thousand members of the State Militia to active service in the Confederate Army and had sent them into battle. On June 17, before Frémont had reached Boston, they had met a Union force under Captain Nathaniel Lyon at Booneville, Missouri, and had been defeated.

Obviously the state, though still officially a part of the Union, was a critical spot. If a Confederate force entered it from the south, it would find friends and recruits awaiting it and might well conquer lower Missouri, take Cairo and the southern part of Illinois, and easily bring the now doubtful Kentucky into the ranks of the rebels. With these things accomplished, victory for the South would seem apparent.

Two key spots were in danger when Frémont took command on July 25: Springfield, Missouri, which General Nathaniel Lyon held with too few troops and inadequately protected communications at his rear; and Cairo, Illinois, where General Benjamin M. Prentiss was threatened by a large Confederate force under Generals Pillow and Hardee.

Immediately on his arrival in St. Louis, Frémont received a frantic appeal for help from Prentiss. "Have but eight regiments here," the message read. "Six of them are three-months men. Their time expires this week —am reorganizing now. I have neither tents nor wagons and must hold Cairo and Bird's Point." Six days later another desperate cry for reinforcements came, and three days later still another.

Frémont found himself working from five in the morning until midnight, day after day, trying to do the impossible. General Lyon and General Prentiss both needed troops, and Frémont had none to send them. Confederate sympathizers in Missouri had begun a troublesome guerrilla warfare which had to be stopped. Volunteers without any training were coming to St. Louis to join the Union Army. They had to be trained and equipped. The large number of Confederate sympathizers in St. Louis had to be kept under control. And Frémont himself was inexperienced in the command of so large a force, as well as in the military tactics and the problems of transportation involved in the kind of operations required by the Civil War.

Clearly he would have to decide whether to help Lyon or Prentiss. It seemed to him that it was far more important to hold Cairo than Springfield. As a matter of fact, President Lincoln had said that Cairo must be held at all costs. The Commander of the Western Army therefore advised Lyon to retreat to his base at Rolla. That done, Frémont worked day and night to get together, provision, and arm a force of four thousand men, and

eight steamboats to take them upriver to Cairo. When
the flotilla reached Cairo, Frémont, who went along with
it, received a salute of guns from the shore batteries, and
rousing cheers from those who met the boats at the
wharf.

Meanwhile Lyon at Springfield refused to follow his
superior's directive to retreat and, when a large Confederate force approached Springfield, went out to meet it.
In the bloody battle of Wilson's Creek, ten miles south of
Springfield, Lyon was killed and the Union forces defeated, with a loss of between twelve and thirteen hundred men. Only now did the remaining forces, under the
command of Colonel Sigel, follow the directive Frémont
had issued earlier, and retreat to Rolla, leaving Springfield to the Confederates.

Though Lyon had done a foolhardy thing, he had
also done an exceedingly courageous one, and had died
a hero's death. As the news of the battle and its disastrous result spread over the country, criticism of Frémont for not having sent reinforcements to Lyon followed in its wake. It was not generally known that he
had no forces to send. Nor did Frémont ever make public the letter in which he had directed Lyon to retreat,
or publicize his reasons for reinforcing Cairo instead of
Springfield. He was too busy policing St. Louis, putting
an end to the recruiting of soldiers for the Confederate
Army, stopping guerrilla warfare, and training recruits
for the Union Army. Day after day the criticism increased. No one not intimately familiar with the situation at St. Louis could understand the chaotic situation

of affairs there—a situation with which the most experienced army man would have found it difficult to deal. Frémont had not enough men, not enough arms, not enough supplies, not enough support from the populace.

At the end of July he sent appeals to the War Department agent in New York and to President Lincoln, begging for arms—"any arms, no matter what." But the War Department, intent on the situation in the East, and itself in short supply of troops and arms, neglected his plea. He continued to work with the energy that had marked his crossing of the Sierras in winter. He had constructed a fortified railroad station on the river to expedite troop movements. He quickly set up a river service, took a census of river boats, and ordered a corps of river men organized. He set up offices in the Brant residence on Chouteau Avenue where he and his staff could work together, and in the basement of which could be stored arms and ammunition against possible emergencies.

But many of these activities were misunderstood and misrepresented by his critics. It was said that he was paying $60,000 a year for a sumptuous mansion in which he surrounded himself with luxury, that he swaggered through the streets with a strong bodyguard, that he had so many sentinels that it was almost impossible to see him, and that if a visitor did manage to meet him, he was treated with coldness and dismissed as quickly as possible. The truth was that, working sometimes eighteen hours or more a day and still finding it impossible to do all that should be done, Frémont sought to save time in every way possible.

One of the greatest of his anxieties arose from the increasing activities of the rebel guerrillas, especially in central and northern parts of the state, where they burned bridges, wrecked railroad trains, made scattered raids on farms, and sudden attacks on small Union Army units.

Frémont decided upon bold punitive measures, without consulting Washington, following his old habit of making and carrying out decisions for himself. On August 30, 1861, nearly two years before Lincoln's Emancipation Proclamation freed the slaves in ten states (not including Missouri), Frémont issued a proclamation freeing the slaves of all "persons in the state of Missouri directly proven to have taken an active part with their enemies in the field." The proclamation also placed the state under martial law, declared that the lines of the Union Army ran from Leavenworth through Jefferson City, Rolla, and Ironton to Cape Girardeau, and that anyone found in possession of arms north of this line would be tried by Court Martial and, if found guilty, shot.

Like so much that Frémont did, the proclamation received enthusiastic approval on the one hand, and violent disapproval on the other. In New England and the Middle West he was loudly praised. All of the dedicated anti-slavery element supported the proclamation heartily. The *Tribune* and *Times* in Chicago, the Boston *Post*, the *Times* in New York, as well as Horace Greeley's *Tribune*, William Cullen Bryant's *Evening Post*, and James Gordon Bennett's *Herald* all praised it. Simon

Cameron, Secretary of War, telegraphed his approval and congratulations to Frémont. Charles Sumner, the Free-Soil-Democratic Senator from Massachusetts, was delighted. In Cincinnati a great mass meeting expressed its feelings with "screaming, yelling, stamping, whooping, throwing hats, and embracing each other." William Lloyd Garrison's *Liberator* called it "the beginning of the end" (of slavery) and added "Laus Deo!" (Praise God!)

But the man whose opinion mattered most, President Lincoln, was not pleased. With courtesy and gentleness typical of the President, he sent a letter to Frémont at once.

Should you shoot a man, according to the proclamation, the Confederates would very certainly shoot our best men in their hands in retaliation; and so, man for man, indefinitely. It is therefore my order that you allow no man to be shot under the proclamation without first having my approbation or consent. . . .

I think there is great danger that the closing paragraph, in relation to the confiscation of property and the liberating slaves of traitorous owners will alarm our Southern Union friends and turn them against us; perhaps ruin our rather fair prospect for Kentucky. Allow me, therefore, to ask that you will, as of your own motion, modify that paragraph so as to conform to the first and fourth sections of the act of Congress entitled "An act to confiscate property used for insurrectionary purposes" approved August 6, 1861, and a copy of which act I herewith send you.

It was a gracious attempt on the part of the President to make it possible for Frémont to save face by voluntarily changing an order rather than doing so as a result of a command from higher authority. But Frémont was firm in his pride. He wrote President Lincoln:

If upon reflection your better judgment still decides that I am wrong in the article respecting the liberation of the slaves, I have to ask that you openly direct me to make the correction. . . . If I were to retract of my own accord, it would imply that I myself thought it wrong, and that I had acted without the reflection which the gravity of the point demanded. But I did not. I acted with full deliberation, and upon the certain conviction that it was a measure right and necessary, and I think so still.

Lincoln was quick to do as Frémont asked. He wrote at once mentioning the clause concerning the liberation of slaves and referring to their earlier correspondence, and continued:

It is therefore ordered that the said clause be so modified, held, and construed as to conform to, and not to transcend, the provisions on the same subject contained in the act of Congress entitled "An act to confiscate property used for insurrectionary purposes. . . ."

This was the beginning of the rift between Frémont and Lincoln that continued to widen and was never actually bridged. And, as happened when the proclamation itself was published, the feelings of those for and against were widely expressed. The country was, in fact, more or less divided into pro-Lincoln-anti-Frémont and pro-Frémont-anti-Lincoln camps, a division that continued and was to become a factor in the 1864 elections.

Typical of the pro-Frémont expressions was a poem by Frémont's friend Whittier:

> *Thy error, Fremont, simply was to act*
> *A brave man's part, without the statesman's tact,*
> *And, taking counsel but of common sense,*
> *To strike at cause as well as consequence.*
> *O, never yet since Roland wound his horn*
> *At Roncesvalles, has a blast been blown*
> *Far-heard, wide-echoing, startling as thine own,*
> *Heard from the van of Freedom's hope forlorn!*
> *It had been safer, doubtless, for the time*
> *To flatter treason, and avoid offense*
> *To that Dark Power whose underlying crime*
> *Heaves upwards its perpetual turbulence.*
> *But if thine be the fate of all who break*
> *The ground for truth's seed, or forerun their years*
> *Till lost in distance or with stout hearts make*
> *A lane for freedom through the level spears,*
> *Still take thou courage! God has spoken through*
> *thee,*
> *Irrevocable, the mighty words, Be free!*

The next act in the grim drama of Frémont's decline and fall in the military service opened with a clash between Frémont and the Blair clan of St. Louis and Washington. The head of the family, Francis Preston

Francis Preston Blair   *Montgomery Blair*

Blair, was a powerful newspaper editor, influential in Washington political circles. A relative of Jessie's, and a friend, he was often her host at his home at Silver Spring, Maryland. One son, Montgomery, was Postmaster General at the time when Frémont was in command of the Western Department of the Army. Another, Francis Preston Jr., commonly called Frank, had been congressman from Missouri and had left his seat there to join the Union Army. Now in St. Louis, he spent much time in Frémont's office, asking for, and usually receiving, favors for friends in the granting of Army contracts. However, as it became clear that Blair intended to dominate the direction of the Army there, Frémont's back stiffened, with the help of Jessie's determined independence. Bit by bit, irritation arose between the two men, which flared into a first-class conflict when Frémont reduced a contract Blair had promised to a friend by cancellation of large parts of it.

Frank immediately wrote to his father complaining of Frémont's lack of cooperation, and the head of the formidable clan wrote Frémont an arrogant, peremptory letter, saying, in part, "I shall expect you to exert your utmost influence to carry my points, and now, to begin, I want to have Frank made a militia major-general for the State of Missouri." This was prefaced by the offer of what, in effect, was a bribe—the assurance that he and his sons would do everything in their power to aid Frémont if he, in turn, would cooperate.

This was the wrong approach to John Charles Frémont, who was not tempted by such promises. He hoped that Frank Blair would go back East and solve the problem by his absence from Missouri. But the elder Blair continued to write letters insisting that Frémont cooperate with his son. When the letters brought no result, a careful program of criticism was begun. Blair condemned as wasteful extravagance the ten forts Frémont had ordered built in St. Louis, and in October the War Department countermanded the orders for them.

The younger Frank Blair's letters from St. Louis, opposing Frémont's proclamation freeing the slaves in Missouri, stirred the anti-Frémont feeling in Washington.

In September President Lincoln sent Montgomery Blair, the Postmaster General, and Montgomery Meigs, the Quartermaster General, to St. Louis to observe and report on the situation there. At the same time, in a letter to General David Hunter at Chicago the President wrote:

> General Frémont . . . is losing the confidence of men near him, whose support any man in his position must have to be successful. His cardinal mistake is that he isolates himself and allows nobody to see him; and by which he does not know what is going on in the very matter he is dealing with.

Clearly the Blair campaign was having its intended influence.

Perhaps Montgomery Blair had decided what his report would be before ever leaving Washington. In any case it surprised no one who knew the intimate details of the Blair-Frémont feud. Frémont was, he said, "a mere trifler." The welfare of the Union cause demanded his removal.

But the Frémonts were not to go down without a furious attempt at justification by the member of the family who was even more militant than Frémont himself. Jessie left St. Louis for Washington in a towering rage, with a letter from her husband to President Lincoln. Both Lincoln and Jessie later reported on their short interview. Though the two reports differed in detail they agreed that there was definitely a cool atmosphere in the room as they talked. Jessie reported that the President's mind was apparently made up against

Frémont and herself before ever she reached Washington. She quoted Lincoln as having said, "General Frémont should not have dragged the Negro into it—he never would have if he had consulted with Frank Blair. I sent Frank there to advise him."

This enraged Jessie still further and she at once sent off a letter to her husband warning him against being fooled by any show of friendship on the part of the Postmaster General, Montgomery Blair, who was apparently using a diplomatic approach in contrast to Frank's bluster. She adds, in her report, that she never spoke to Montgomery Blair again.

The next scene was set against a military background. Frémont had placed a recently made brigadier general named Ulysses S. Grant in command of the Union forces in southeastern Missouri and southern Illinois. A few days before Jessie had started for Washington, Grant had taken Paducah, Kentucky, at the junction of the Tennessee and Ohio rivers, an important point on the way to the Mississippi, the control of which might well decide the issue of the war. Though Grant acted on his own initiative, without consulting Frémont, Frémont had made the action possible by diverting troops from Missouri to the Paducah area. It was this movement that he had reported in the letter Jessie carried to President Lincoln. He also outlined, in his letter, a plan to advance upon Nashville and Memphis, Tennessee.

But troops cannot be in two places at the same time, and Frémont simply did not have enough men to keep every vital point under his command strong. When Colonel Mulligan, stationed at Lexington in northwest Missouri, learned that a strong force of Confederates was marching toward him, he appealed frantically to Frémont for reinforcements. But there were none to send him. At about the same time—on September 14—a telegram from Secretary of War Cameron said that the President had directed him to call on Frémont for "five thousand well armed infantry, to be sent without a moment's delay." Another telegram from General Winfield Scott on the same day read "Detach five thousand infantry from your department to come here without delay and report the number of troops that will be left with you."

Later, when Frémont was being hotly criticized for not having gone to Mulligan's relief, he revealed that at the time he had had only 6,890 men at his disposal in St. Louis, including the home guard, and several incomplete and untrained units. This force was not even strong enough to defend St. Louis itself in case of attack.

On September 18 the Confederate General Price, at the head of vastly superior forces, attacked Mulligan's troops at Lexington. On the twentieth, the Union troops were forced to surrender. Again Frémont was hotly criticized by his opponents who did not know how scanty his resources were, or that he had telegraphed in vain to Generals Pope, Sturgis, and Davis, at various locations in his command, directing them to march to the relief of Lexington. They could not spare troops either.

Among the totally unfair blasts directed at Frémont were malignant letters such as the one that appeared in the *National Intelligencer,* signed simply "A Missourian," and possibly written by Frank Blair. Why, it asked, did not Frémont use some of his "60,000 splendidly equipped soldiers to drive the confederates out of the state?" He was criticized for the five hundred tons of ice that he had requisitioned because hospitals in his command had requested it. But his detractors assumed that the ice was for the personal use of Frémont and his officers. It was said that he had surrounded himself with a group of grafting confidence men and was turning his back on their thievery. Frank Blair and others accused him of what, had it been true, would have amounted to treason —a plan to set up an independent military republic in the West.

At this point Frémont lost patience and placed Frank Blair under arrest, charging, as he reported to Washington, "insidious and dishonorable efforts to bring my authority into contempt with the government and so to undermine my influence as an officer." Though Blair was soon released, the bitter animosity between him and Frémont never died, and the event itself increased the cleavage between the pro-Frémont and the anti-Frémont groups throughout the country.

Frémont, realizing that his reputation was being damaged and that the repeated defeats of the Northern forces were becoming alarming, sent word to General Winfield Scott, the Supreme Commander of the Union Army, "I am taking the field myself and hope to destroy the enemy. . . . Please notify the President immediately."

His plan was to concentrate five divisions on Lexington to retake it, and then pursue the retreating Confederate General Price. He ordered five commanders—Pope, McKinstry, Hunter, Sigel, and Asboth—to march to the site of the forthcoming siege. But the divisions were without adequate transportation and supplies, and the whole program lagged.

Meanwhile President Lincoln was beginning to believe that those who demanded Frémont's removal were right, and sent Secretary of War Simon Cameron, accompanied by Adjutant General Lorenzo Thomas, to have a talk with Frémont, to consider his plans and the conduct of his program on the spot, and to act according to his own judgment. Cameron was given an order for Frémont's removal to be used if it seemed advisable. This order he showed to the Pathfinder, who begged him not to act at once, but to wait and see what the results of the campaign against Lexington were. If that was not successful, he promised to resign immediately. With this promise, Cameron went back to Washington, and the dismissal order was temporarily stayed.

But not for long. On returning to Washington, Adjutant General Thomas, who had been strongly influenced in his talks with the Blairs at St. Louis, had made a report of his own, saying that Frémont was incompetent, extravagant, and guilty of financial irregularities in the handling of government funds. This opinion was supported by reports from General Hunter and Brigadier General Curtis, stationed in St. Louis, both of whom charged him with incompetence. Elihu P. Washburne, U.S. Representative from Illinois, following a visit to St.

Louis, reported that a "horde of pirates" were handling government affairs there and that "such robbery, fraud, extravagance, peculation as have developed in Frémont's department can hardly be conceived of."

It was inevitable that the anti-Frémont forces, with the Blairs in the van, should influence President Lincoln. On November 2, Frémont, in his camp near Springfield, was busily planning an advance and probably an engagement with Price's forces the next day, when a messenger arrived bearing an order from the President, relieving the Pathfinder of his command, which he was to turn over to General Hunter.

The news spread quickly throughout the camp and his loyal men were aghast. Many of them threw down their arms, saying that they would not fight under any leader other than Frémont. Many officers declared that they would resign. Some even threatened to resist General Hunter by force when he arrived. Calmly, the General went from one group of excited men to another, quieting them and reminding them that their duty was to the United States of America, and not to any individual officer. "It would be impossible to exaggerate the gloom which pervaded our camp," the New York *Herald's* correspondent reported, "and nothing but General Frémont's urgent endeavors prevented it from ripening into a general mutiny."

Frémont handed over his command to Hunter late that night and returned to St. Louis, where he was met with bands and a great mass of cheering people. Throughout the city flags were at half-mast or draped in black, as a protest against his removal. He was amazed to learn that many soldiers had declared they were through with the war. Special guards had been appointed for Frank Blair because of threats to lynch him.

The storm of protest spread throughout the country. The Cincinnati *Gazette* asked editorially,

Is it known that the West is threatened with a revolution? Could you have been among the people yesterday and witnessed the excitement; could you have seen sober citizens pulling from their walls and trampling under foot the portrait of the President; and could you hear today the expressions of all classes of men, of all political parties, you would, I think, feel as I feel, as every sincere friend of the government must feel, alarmed.

Henry Ward Beecher asked Frémont to come to Plymouth Church one Sunday morning, where, speaking directly to him, Beecher said, "Your name will live and be remembered by a nation of freemen."

And in 1863 a semi-official justification of his conduct, which amounted almost to a public apology by the government, came in the verdict of a Congressional Committee on the Conduct of the War, which absolved him from blame for not having reinforced Lyon or Mulligan, and said that his conduct "was eminently characterized by earnestness, ability, and the most unquestionable loyalty."

Disaster

✠

OLLOWING the Presidential election of 1856, what was left of the shattered Whig Party had followed the "Know-Nothings" or American Party, the Free Soilers, and the Liberty Party into the vigorous young Republican Party, greatly adding to its strength. Four years later, in 1860, the Democratic Party was torn by inner dissension and formed three splinter groups, each with a different Presidential candidate. Thus weakened, they were easily defeated by the Republicans, who elected Abraham Lincoln.

The next great political crisis came with the Presidential election of 1864. Meanwhile the Lincoln-Frémont feud, and the military setbacks that the Union armies had suffered, had turned many former supporters against the President. Lincoln's attempt to placate the wrath of those who censured him by giving Frémont a new assignment as Commandant of the Mountain Department in Western Virginia resulted only in further conflict between them, and the General soon asked Lincoln to relieve him of his command. His request was immediately granted.

As the time for the 1864 nominating convention approached several ambitious politicians attempted to take advantage of the disfavor into which Lincoln had fallen in so many quarters. Opposition to the President became more intense as his critics became more voluble. Edwin Stanton, whom Lincoln had made Secretary of War in 1862, spoke openly of the President's "painful imbecility." James A. Garfield, then a representative from Ohio, strongly opposed the President. Salmon P. Chase, Lincoln's Secretary of the Treasury, sought the nomination in the hope of displacing Lincoln.

Henry Ward Beecher's *Independent*, James Gordon Bennett's *Herald*, Greeley's *Tribune*, Bryant's *Evening Post*, the Cincinnati *Gazette*, and other papers strongly attacked Lincoln and prophesied dire tragedy for the country if he was re-elected.

The Republicans who opposed the re-election of Lincoln naturally began to think once more about Frémont as a candidate. Though he had been beaten eight years before, they believed that this time they might be able to elect him. It is doubtful that the Pathfinder was particularly eager to run. Having decided that he wanted no more connection with the Army, he had become absorbed in a project to build a railroad across the state of Kansas, to be called The Leavenworth, Pawnee, and Western. The board of directors had been chosen and Frémont elected president. While his supporters were urging his nomination, he was busy in an office on Beaver Street, New York, considering bids for four hundred tons of iron rails.

But if he desired to stay out of politics, there were those who decided that he was not to be allowed to do so. When, on February 22, the Republican nominating committee made it clear that Lincoln would be nominated, Eastern Abolitionists, impatient because the President had not yet come out strongly for the emancipation of the slaves, called a "Frémont meeting" at Cooper Union in New York, urging that the Pathfinder be asked to run on a third party ticket.

On May 31, a convention of delegates from sixteen states met at Cleveland and nominated him. Once more the man who had been the Republican Party's first Presidential candidate was running for the highest office in the land, but not as the choice of the regular Republican Party. That honor was awarded, as everyone knew it would be, to Abraham Lincoln, at Baltimore in June.

Apparently Frémont did not give much attention to his campaign. The new railroad through Kansas interested him more, and the regular Republicans at first thought of his candidacy as something that need not be taken seriously. At the beginning of the summer, Lincoln's popularity had increased, following greater displays of strength on the part of the Union armies. But as the tide of battle turned against the North once more in July and August, harsh voices were again raised against the President. It became known that so great was the prospect that Southern forces would take Washington, that a special ship was held ready on the Potomac for Lincoln's escape. A Northern paper dollar became worth about forty cents, and Northern gloom blamed

Lincoln for all misfortunes. By the middle of August, well-informed leaders of the Republican Party said that if an election were held right then, the Democrats would win a large victory.

The dissatisfaction with Lincoln brought about greater pressure for Frémont's election, and the regular Republicans began to take the Pathfinder's candidacy seriously. Even if he did not win the election, they saw that the votes cast for him would be votes lost to Lincoln, and that the result would, therefore, be a Democratic victory.

This was the state of affairs when Zachariah Chandler, Republican senator from Michigan, called on Frémont in New York. Bluntly he told the Pathfinder that Lincoln would not withdraw from the Presidential campaign, but that if both he and Frémont were still candidates on election day there was no doubt whatever that the election would be lost to the Democrats. However, the Senator continued, the President had authorized him to tell Frémont that if he would withdraw he would be given a high command in the Army, with active service at once, and that the Blairs would be placed in a position that would make it impossible for them to make further trouble. When this suggestion was rejected, Frémont was offered a cabinet post. He asked for a week in which to consider the matter.

Meanwhile he asked friends, whose judgment he respected, for advice. Wendell Phillips advised him to stay in the race. But John Greenleaf Whittier, pointing out how disastrous a change of leaders in the midst of war would be, asked him to abandon his candidacy for the good of the country. What offers of an Army command and a cabinet post could not do, the gentle and wise words of a Quaker friend did, and he consented to withdraw his name, though not without some bitterness. "I consider," he wrote of Lincoln, "his administration has been politically, militarily, and financially a failure, and that its necessary continuance is a cause of regret for this country."

Later Jessie wrote Whittier, "I shall never forget your words, 'There is a time to do and a time to stand aside . . . renounce self for the good of the greater number.' Do you not remember it too? It was a deciding word coming from you."

Now Frémont could forget both politics and a military career. He had taken a fortune in gold out of the Mariposa estate, but he had never known how to conserve his money, nor had he the kind of business judgment that was necessary for handling investments wisely. Though his tastes in clothing and food were simple, he lived like the millionaire that he was—with a large brownstone mansion on west Nineteenth Street between Fifth and Sixth Avenues in Manhattan, and an estate consisting of more than a hundred acres of lawn and woodland about two miles north of Tarrytown, New York. (The house in San Francisco had been commandeered by the government for military use in the war. It was never returned to Frémont, nor was he ever compensated for it.) An adequate staff of servants made entertainment in the Frémont home a gracious affair. He kept a fine horse in New York and often rode in Central Park. Tutors were engaged for the children, and Lilly drove a pair of her own horses.

But these expenditures made it impossible to maintain a sound financial position for the Mariposa holdings. In 1862, his indebtedness for operations on the California estate totaled about $1,250,000. The interest was about $13,000 a month. The trip that he made to Europe in 1861, which was interrupted by the outbreak of the war, had been undertaken for the purpose of selling a half interest in the estate, or, if he was unable to do this, to obtain a loan at more favorable interest rates than those he was currently paying. Though he talked with the Rothschilds in London and with bankers in Paris, he was unsuccessful in both efforts.

Now, in 1863, in an attempt to bring some order into the Mariposa tangle, a corporation was formed and stock was sold. Frémont was left owning only three-eighths of the property, and had to pay legal expenses of $600,000. And this was not the end of his Mariposa misfortunes. According to Jessie's later accounts, those who held the rest of the stocks did everything in their power to embarrass her husband in order to get him to withdraw from the enterprise. Litigation hampered productive activities. The very expensive dam across the Merced River was swept away, and both Frémont and Jessie believed that it happened because the man in charge had deliberately neglected to open the sluice gates in flood time.

Finally he gave up and sold his shares in the Mariposa venture. Though he now had only a fraction of the large fortune he had possessed a few years before, he was still a rich man, and he and Jessie would have been quite secure if he had invested his money in securities that had been proved sound. But railroad fever was in his blood, and all of the money he had went into railroad speculation. A small railroad across Kansas was not enough. He would span with rails the continent he had crossed so laboriously on foot and horse- or mule-back. He began to buy up small railway projects or parts of them—the Kansas Pacific, and an interest in the Memphis and El Paso, of which he became president. He induced California, Arizona, and Arkansas to issue franchises, and bought 9,000 acres of land near San Diego which was to be the Pacific terminal of the line that was to fulfill his dream of a coast-to-coast railroad over a more hospitable, because more southerly, route than that being followed by the rapidly building Union Pacific to the north. Fifty miles of track were laid, locomotives were ordered, surveyors were at work in the West, over five million dollars worth of bonds were sold in Europe.

And then the blow fell. Money for the bonds sold in Europe came in slowly, and two-fifths of it was retained by the agents who arranged the sales. The cost of grading and the difficulties of transportation were far greater than had been anticipated. The company could not pay its bills and, in 1870, following an application by the holders of mortgages, the Federal government ordered the properties seized.

Frémont always threw everything he had into any effort he made. So it had been with his railroading venture, and now he had almost literally nothing. In only a few years, the millionaire had become practically a pauper. The house on West Nineteenth Street in New York had to go. The fine estate north of Tarrytown, with its expansive lawns and green forests, went; the horses, most of the paintings and objects of art, the books, and other valuable and treasured personal possessions—souvenirs of Washington, California, Paris. For a time even the family had to be separated, Jessie accepting the hospitality of one friend, Frémont staying with another.

Over and over during his career as an explorer Frémont had proved his courage. Not even the most vicious of those who had been his critics in the past could ever charge him with cowardice. But never—not even in the worst moments of near despair during his wintry struggles over the pathless Sierra—had he needed greater courage than now. He was nearing sixty in 1870, he had three still dependent children, and he was without money and even without a home. But he still had his courage and held his head high. And beside him stood the one who for nearly forty years had shared his triumphs and successes, as well as his fears and defeats. She had hurried to his aid, gone to his defense, waited patiently for months without word from him when he was on his dangerous Western expeditions. With courage as great as his own, Jessie now rallied to the difficult task of saving what could be saved from the wreckage of the Frémont fortunes.

The End of a Long Trail

✠

AFTER THE COLLAPSE of Frémont's fortune
the immediate need was, of course, for someone
in the family to begin making money, and without hesitation Jessie set out to do so. Very quickly she obtained an
agreement from the New York *Ledger* to pay her $100
each for a series of articles that she wrote rapidly. Articles for several magazines followed. She wrote stories for
children that were published in *Wide Awake,* various
articles for the *Ledger,* some historical pieces for the
Century. Collections of some of the magazine pieces
appeared in books: *A Year of American Travel, Far West
Sketches, The Will and the Way Stories,* the last a book
for children, and *Souvenirs of My Time.*

Her husband was, meanwhile, until March 1878,
helping the receivers of the Memphis and El Paso Railroad to straighten out the tangled affairs of that defunct
enterprise. His salary was not sufficient to support him
and his family in the small cottage on Staten Island that
had replaced their two former stately homes.

The situation was somewhat relieved when President
Hayes, acting on the suggestion of Zachariah Chandler

and other friends, appointed Frémont Territorial Governor of Arizona. The salary was small, but the position at least gave the Pathfinder an opportunity to follow once more the trail westward which he had blazed, to see the West again, and to visit some old friends. Once located at Prescott, the territorial capital, he spent much time in the saddle, living the outdoor life he loved. Busying himself with large ideas of projects to improve the desert region—such as flooding a large sunken area in California by diverting the Colorado River through it, planning possible reservoirs to be used for irrigation, developing mining areas, and building railroads, he found comfort for the wounds suffered in the wrecks of his political, his military, and his financial careers.

But poverty hung like a dark cloud over all thoughts of the future and, in 1883, hoping to establish himself in business in New York, he resigned his post and the Frémonts returned to their small house on Staten Island. Here Frémont attempted to rouse the interest of several English capitalists in some of the projects that had appealed to him in Arizona—especially in various mining enterprises—but had no success.

Visitors to the Frémont home had to look beneath the surface to discover how poor they were. Neither by word or act did either of them intimate the true state of their affairs. The few paintings they had left from the financial debacle, the bric-a-brac of which they were especially fond, several medals from foreign governments, the flag he had flown from Frémont's Peak, and the campaign banners from 1856 were all proudly displayed. Jessie remained the gracious hostess, the graying Frémont the dignified host and gentleman.

Jessie continued to earn a little money writing, and now Frémont turned to the same occupation, writing *Memoirs of My Life, a Retrospect of Fifty Years*. It was intended to be a two-volume work, but not enough copies of the first volume were sold to encourage the publisher, and the second volume was never published.

And then came a new discouragement. In 1887 Frémont contracted bronchitis. His illness hung on so long and was so severe that his physician said that he must go to a warmer climate.

Once more Jessie stepped into the breech. Swallowing her pride, she went to an old friend, Collis P. Huntington, one of the organizers and builders of the Central Pacific and Southern Pacific Railroads, and told him the whole story. She found a sympathetic ear and a generous heart awaiting her.

"He must go to California," Huntington exclaimed. "He would have my private car if I had not already lent it to someone else."

In lieu of his private car, he furnished the next best thing. That night, he himself brought Frémont Pullman tickets, letters to railroad officials along the way, and a generous sum of money which he insisted, against Frémont's protests, should be taken for their expenses. The next day they were on their way westward and they had not been out of New York twenty-four hours before Frémont told Jessie that he was feeling better.

Perhaps it was as a result of their crossing the Rocky

Mountains by train on this trip that Frémont wrote the poem, "On Crossing the Rocky Mountains After Many Years"—if indeed it was he who wrote it. It is included under this title in *Songs of Three Centuries,* edited by Whittier, but ascribed to an unknown author. However, a list of Frémont items penned in the back of a copy of the Upham biography by an obviously careful recorder attributes the verses firmly to Frémont. Every other notation in the list is accurate. Though Frémont is not known as a poet, it will be remembered that Dr. John Robertson, his teacher in preparatory school, had revealed how the boy, at fourteen, had written creditable verse that was published in a Charleston newspaper. The phrases "a score of horsemen," and "the midsummer of the year" may have referred to the summer expedition of 1842 which consisted of twenty-three men when the party crossed the Rockies. It seems likely that Frémont wrote the poem and sent it to his friend Whittier. When Whittier proposed to include the poem in his anthology, Frémont may have asked modestly that his name be withheld. The lines sound like Frémont, and reflect what must have been his emotions at this time (four verses have been omitted):

> *Long years ago I wandered here*
> *In the midsummer of the year—*
> *Life's summer, too;*
> *A score of horsemen here we rode*
> *The mountain world its glories showed,*
> *All fair to view.*

Now changed the scene and changed the eyes,
That here once looked on glowing skies,
Where summer smiled.
These riven trees, this wind-swept plain,
Now show the winter's dread domain,
Its fury wild.

The buoyant hopes and busy life
Have ended all in hateful strife
*   and thwarted aim.*
The world's rude contact killed the rose,
No more its radiant color shows
False roads to fame.

Backwards amidst the twilight glow
Some lingering spots yet brightly show
On hard roads won,
Where still some grand peaks mark the way
Touched by the light of parting day
And memory's sun.

But here thick clouds the mountains hide,
The dim horizon dark and wide
No pathway shows,
And rising gusts, and darkening sky
Tell of "the night that cometh" nigh,
The brief day's close.

Frémont's rest in California improved his health so
greatly that in 1889 he returned alone to New York,

leaving Jessie in California. He was once again hoping for a business connection that would enable him to maintain a dignified financial position.

In April 1890, Congress restored Frémont's rank of major general and awarded him the pension of a retired officer of that rank—$6,000 a year. This removed his financial worries.

But he was not to enjoy the sense of security long. Having become overheated and fatigued on a hot July day, he became ill in the night and, on July 13, died.

Before the end of that year, a group of friends and admirers presented Jessie with a cottage in a good residential part of Los Angeles. At the same time, Congress passed a bill awarding her a pension of $2,000 a year as the widow of a major general, and she lived in Los Angeles in comparative comfort until December 27, 1902, when she died.

A list of the tributes paid to Frémont during his life and after his death would fill many pages. Some remembered the little things that perhaps are more important than the seemingly larger things, for they tell so much of a man's inner nature. His son, for instance, remembered how he had loved trees, and refused to have any cut down on his property unless it was absolutely necessary, and then insisted upon doing the job himself—as if he were afraid that a clumsy hand would actually give the trees pain. He told, too, how, riding in Arizona, his father would often turn his horse so that he would avoid stepping on a flower or an ant hill. All life had been precious to him. The son also told how his father once had stayed his impulsive boyish hand when he had started to kill a snake.

Alexander Godey, who had been through so much with him, spoke of Frémont's "daring energy, his indomitable perseverance, and his goodness of heart."

Kit Carson wrote in his autobiography before Frémont's death:

I was with Frémont from 1842 to 1847. I find it impossible to describe the hardships through which we passed, nor am I capable of doing justice to the credit which he deserves. But his services to his country have been left to the judgment of impartial freemen, and have resounded to his honor, and to that of his country. . . .

All that he has or may ever receive he deserves. I can never forget his treatment of me while I was in his employ, and how cheerfully he suffered with his men when undergoing the severest hardships. His perseverance, and his willingness to participate in all that was undertaken, no matter whether the duty was rough or easy, are the main causes of his success; and I say without fear of contradiction, that no one but he could have surmounted so many obstacles and have succeeded in as many difficult services.

But perhaps the most fitting tribute—the more impressive because it is so short—was paid him by Jessie, who wrote: ". . . from the ashes of his campfires have sprung cities."

Index

✠

Abert, Col. J. J., 73–74
Abert, Lt., 120
Abolitionists, 211, 238
Adams, Hull, 19
Altamonte, General, 133
American Fur Co., 28, 32, 35
American Party, 236
Antelope, 32, 34
Arapaho, 80
Astor, John Jacob, 29, 69
astronomical calculations, 13–14, 32, 44, 110
Aubrey, Francis, 179

Badeau, François, 104
Bancroft, George, 151, 153
Banks, Nathaniel P., 203
barometer, *see under* Frémont
Beale, Major Edward F., 178–179
bear, *see under* Frémont
Bear flag, 146
Beecher, Henry Ward, 205, 235, 237
Bennett, James Gordon, 223, 237
Bent's Fort, 87, 115, 120
Benton, Jessie, 45–48; see also Frémont, Jessie
Benton, Randolph, 45; on Frémont expedition, 50, 51, 54, 58
Benton, Sarah, 45
Benton, Thomas Hart, 44; plans of, for settling of West, 44, 49, 68-69, 85; objects to marriage, 46–48; goes to St. Louis, 70; and howitzer, 74; and deacon, 110–111; and California, 132; letters to, from Frémont, 140, 148, 156, 177, 199; at Court Martial, 164; and Frémont campaign, 210; death of, 213
Benton, Mrs. Thomas Hart, 45, 46–48, 70–71, 201

Bigelow, John, 203, 204
Blackfeet, 56
Blair, Francis Preston, 193, 226–227; and Frémont campaign, 204; letters of, to Frémont, 228
Blair, Francis Preston Jr., 227–228, 230, 232, 235
Blair, Montgomery, 227–230
Bois-Brulés, 41–42
Brady, Mathew, 200
Brant, Henry, 51, 54, 58
Brant, Sarah Benton, 51, 71
Breckinridge, John C., 204
Bridger, Jim, 56, 58
Bryant, William Cullen, 203–205, 223, 237
Buchanan, James, 142; presidential campaign of, 204, 205, 207; election of, 211
buffalo, 35–36, 40–42, 55, 81

California, problems of, 92, 93, 112, 115, 132, 133, 143; Frémont in, 126–132, 144–161, 182–185, 187–191, 200, 212–215, 246–248, *see also* Mariposa; Bear flag of, 146; becomes part of U.S., 153, 154; constitution of, 185; becomes state, 185, 186; growth of, 187; *see also* Congress *and* slavery
Cameron, Simon, 223–224, 231, 233
Campbell, Archie, 19
Carnero Pass, 170, 197
Carson, Kit, description of, 51–53; Frémont quote about, 52; on first expedition, 53–55, 56, 58, 60, 67; makes will, 56; and 2nd expedition, 71, 78, 83, 91, 102–103, 104–105; becomes farmer, 118–119;

251

and 3rd expedition, 119, 121, 131; and Indian woman, 121; and fight with Indians, 134, 135, 138, 139, 140; on Indian arrows, 136; sent to Washington, 153; with Kearny, 155; and 4th expedition, 169, 179; quote from, on Frémont, 250

Carvallo, S. N., and 5th expedition, 195, 196–197 (quote from), 198, 200

Castro, Don José, and Frémont, 128, 129, 182; and Indians, 142, 143, 145; and Mexican War, 144–145, 146, 149, 153

Cathcart, Capt., 169

Catlin, George, 30

Chandler, Zachariah, 239, 244

Charleston, S. C., 10–11, 15–16

Charleston College, 12–13, 15, 18

Chase, Salmon P., 203, 237

Chavez, Lt., 128

Cherokees, 19

Cheyenne, 56, 80

Childs, J. B., 75

Chinook, 87, 109, 115

Chouteau and Co., 26, 28, 51

Cincinnati *Gazette*, 235, 237

Civil War, 200, 238; beginning of, 216; Frémont and, 216–235; battles of, 219, 221, 230, 231; *see also* Emancipation Proclamation, Lincoln, *and commanders of*

Cochetope Pass, 198

Columbia River, 69, 84–85

Confederate Army, and Missouri, 218–221; *see also* Civil War, battles of, *and names of commanders*

Congress, and Frémont, 68, 111, 193, 216, 235, 249; and Texas, 111–112, 133; and California, 112, 187–188; and Indian beef, 188–189, 193, 200; *see also* United States

Cooper Union, 238

Cosumne Indians, 175–176

Crane, and Indian fight, 135–137

Creutzfeldt, 174

Curtis, Brigadier General, 233

Davis, Jefferson, 186, 194, 218

Dayton, W. L., 203, 204

Delawares, and expeditions, 73, 115, 124, 126, 127, 131, 195–197; and fight with Klamaths, 135–137, 139

Democrats, and Frémont, 201–202, 209; presidential candidates of, 204, 209; dissension among, 236; and slavery, *see* slavery

Denny, murder of, 135–137

De Rosier, 72

Dixon, William, 35, 40

Dodson, Jacob, 70

Donelson, Andrew J., 204

duel, *see under* Frémont

Emancipation Proclamation, 223; Frémont's, 223–226

Emerson, Ralph Waldo, 205

emigrant trains, 75–76, 80–81, 82, 180

Emory, Lt. William F., 157

Eugénie, Empress, 193

Far West Sketches, 244

Faribault, Jean Baptiste, 31

Fillmore, Millard, 204, 210, 211

Fitzpatrick, Thomas, 50, 71–72, 96

Flores, Capt. José Maria, 154

Fort Laramie, 54, 56, 67

Fort Pierre, 34–35

Fort Snelling, 28–29

Fort Sumter, firing on, 216

Fort Vancouver, 85

Fox, Charles Douglas, 213, 214

Free Soilers, 185, 203–204, 236

Frémont, Anne Beverly, 193

Frémont, Elizabeth Benton, *see* Frémont, Lilly

Frémont, Frank Preston, 200, 213

Frémont, Jessie, children of, 67, 167, 189, 193, 200, *see also names of*; reunion of, with husband, 67, 106–109, 162, 182; and reports of expeditions, 68, 110, 171, 173–178; goes to St. Louis, 70; and howitzer, 72–74; quotes from, 74, 192, 202, 218, 230, 250; and Kearny, 166; trip of, to California, 167–169, 181–182; illness of, 181, 186, 191; and Mariposa, 184, 241; and burning of

Index

home, 189–191; and Frémont biography, 204; and Blairs, 227–228, 229; and Lincoln, 229–230; and Huntington, 246; reaction of, to poverty, 243–244, 245–246; as writer, 244, 246; as widow, and death of, 249; tribute from, to Frémont, 250; *see also* Benton, Jessie

Frémont, John Charles, father of, 9–11; mother of, 10–11, 21, 43, 163; birth of, 10; childhood and young manhood of, 11–15; characteristics, interests, and emotions of, 11–15, 17–18, 27, 32, 46, 58, 59–62, 67, 108, 121, 148, 240, 242, 243, 245–246, 249–250; books read by, 12–14; quotes about, 12–13, 149–150, 150–151, 196, 202, 231, 235, 250, *see also* Whittier, poems of; and Cecilia, 14–15; as teacher, 15–17; and duel, 17–18; and Indians, 19–20, 27, 29–31, 40–42, 54, 56, 58, 73, 76, 79–80, 83–84, 86–92, 93–94, 95, 97, 101–104, 109, 115, 121–127, 131, 134–143, 174, 176; as surveyor, 18–20, 47, 184; receives Army commission, 21, 216; and Nicollet expeditions, 26–42, 43–44, 47; lost on prairie, 38; quotes from, 46, 52, 55, 58, 61, 61–62; 67, 71, 72, 80, 82, 83, 84–85, 90, 95, 101, 109, 121–124, 130, 132, 137, 139, 140, 142–143, 148, 152, 156, 158, 166, 171, 173, 174, 175–177, 178, 184, 199, 203, 225, 232, 240, *see also* Memoirs; sent to Iowa, 47; 1st expedition of, 49–67, 68, 111; and Kit Carson, 51, 53, 58, 104–105; 119, 175, *see also* Carson, Kit; and barometer, 59–60; 2nd expedition of, 70–105, 109–111, 113; and howitzer, 71, 72–74, 80, 87–88, 91, 93; and bears, 77–78, 129–130; rumors of disappearance of, 107–109; promotions of, 114, 152, 216; 3rd expedition of, 114–132; and Mexicans and Mexican War, 114, 127–134, 144–154; and Kearny and Stockton, 157–161; Marcy

and, 160; and Mason, 160–161; arrest of, 161, 162; honors, gifts, and tributes to, 162, 163–164, 186, 200, 249–250; Court Martial of, 164–166; 4th expedition of, 168–179; illness of, 186, 195, 246; and beef, 188–189, 193, 200; burning of home of, 189–191; and English immigrants, 190–191; debts of, 193, 241; 5th expedition of, 194–200; and prairie fire, 196–197; biographies of, 204, 247; niece of (Nina), 213; and poverty, 243–244, 245–246; becomes Territorial Governor of Arizona, 245; becomes writer, 246; poem by (quoted), 247–248; death of, 249; and Jessie, *see* Benton, Jessie *and* Frémont, Jessie; children of, *see under* Frémont, Jessie; homes of, *see* Mariposa, California, New York, Tarrytown, Staten Island; and slavery, *see* slavery; and Lincoln, *see* Lincoln; and Civil War, *see* Civil War; clash of, with Blairs, *see names of Blairs; see also* astronomical calculations, buffalo, Charleston College, Emancipation Proclamation, map-making, railroads, St. Louis, Washington, D.C., *and names of friends and associates*

Frémont, John Charles III, 189, 213
Frémont, Lilly, 67, 70, 109, 110, 181, 211, 213, 214, 241
Frémont Peak, 59–61, 62–63
Frenière, Louison, 35
Fuentes, Andres, 101–102
Fugitive Slave Law, 201
Fuller, Oliver, 199

Garde, Comte de la, 192
Garfield, James A., 237
Garrison, William Lloyd, 211
Geyer, Charles, 28
Gillespie, Lt. Archibald, 131–134; and Mexican War, 148, 151, 152, 154
Godey, Alexander, and 2nd expedition, 102–103; and 3rd expedition,

115, 124, 126, 131; and Indian women, 124, 126; and Mexican War, 152, 154; and 4th expedition, 169, 174, 176; tribute to Frémont from, 250

gold, discovery of, 180, 182, 183; see also Mariposa

Grant, Ulysses S., 230

Gray, Capt. Robert, 69

Great Britain, and Columbia River, 69; and California, 93, 112, 132; and Oregon, 112; and Texas, 133; and Indians, 140, 142

Greeley, Horace, 205, 215, 223, 237

Gregorio, 109, 115

Gwynn, William, 185

Hardee, Gen'l William J., 219

Harper's Magazine, 52–53

Harrison, William, 46

Hassler, Ferdinand, 44, 46, 109

Hayes, Rutherford B., 244

Hernandez, Pablo, 101–102, 109

History of the People of the U.S.A., quote from, 23

Hornitas League, 213–214

Horse Thief Indians, 126–127

Houston, Sam, 111

Howard, John R., 213

howitzer, see under Frémont

Hubbard, Joseph, 110, 176

Hunter, Gen'l David, 229, 233, 234

Huntington, Collis P., 246

Hurst, Decatur, and duel, 17–18

Ide, William B., 145–146

Independent, The, 209, 237

Indians, moving of, and resistance to, 19; feasts of, 19, 20, 58; in St. Louis, 27–28; villages of, 29, 89, 91–92, 126; at Pipestone, 30; and howitzer, 80, 88; and Sierras, 86, 89–90, 93–94, 95–96; from Sutter's Fort, 97–98; attack by, 101–104; inciting of, 128, 140, 142, 145; at Mariposa, 179; and beef, 188–189, 193, 200; see also names of tribes

Irving, Washington, 205

Jackson, Claiborne F., 219

Jackson, David E., 50

Jefferson, Thomas, 10, 19, 22–23

Jones, William Carey, 164

Juan, 109, 115

Kansas Landing, 51, 73, 75, 104, 161, 162; description of, 72; see also Westport Landing

Kansas-Nebraska Act, 201

Kearny, Stephen W., 71, 134, 218; and Stockton, 154, 155–156, 158–159; and Carson, 155; and Frémont, 157–167; death of, 166

Kentucky, and Civil War, 219

Kern, Edward M., and 3rd expedition, 121; in Mexican War, 149; and brothers of, and 4th expedition, 169, 176, 179

King, and 4th expedition, 169, 174

Klamath Indians, 88–89, 134–143

Lajeunesse, Basil, on 1st expedition, 65–66; on 2nd expedition, 71, 83; and 3rd expedition, 115, 131; murder of, 134–138

Lake Klamath, 87, 88, 130–131, 133

Larkin, Thomas O., 167, 179

Lawrence, Abbot, Mr. & Mrs., 192

Lincoln, Abraham, as vice-presidential candidate, 203; and Frémont, 205, 215–217, 222, 224–226, 228–230, 233, 234, 236, 239–240; and Presidency, 215, 236, 238–239; and Cairo, 220; quotes from, 224–225, 229; and Jessie, 229–230; and Blairs, 228–230, 239; criticism of, and opposition to, 234–239

London, Frémonts in, 192, 217, 241

Long, Stephen, 68

Longfellow, Henry W., 205

Louisiana Purchase, 22–26

Lyon, Gen'l Nathaniel, 219, 220, 235; death of, 221

McDowell, James, 120

McGehee, Micajah, 169, 179

McMaster, John B., quote from, 23

map-making, 13–14, 26, 27, 32, 43–44, 47, 48, 110

Marcy, W. L., 160

Index

Mariposa Ranch, 167, 179, 180, 182–183, 187–189, 191, 193, 200, 201, 212–216, 241–242; gold on, 183–185, 215

Maxwell, Lucien, and 1st expedition, 54, 55; and 2nd expedition, 76; and 3rd expedition, 126–127; and fight with Klamaths, 139; aids Frémont, 179

Meigs, Montgomery, 228–229

Memoirs of My Life, 246; quotes from, 13, 15, 20, 31, 36, 40–41, 42, 63–65, 66, 71, 77, 81–82; and Beautiful Day, 29

Merritt, Ezekiel, 148–149

Mexico, and California, 92, 133; U.S. and, 111, 134, 143, 144–154; and Indians, 128, 142, 143; and Texas, 133

Missouri, and Civil War, 218–219

Mitchell, John W., 11

Monterey, 149, 151, 182

Montgomery, John B., 148, 149

Morgan, Edwin D., 204

Mulligan, Col., 230–231, 235

Murchison, Roderick, 192

Napoleon, Louis, 192–193

Natchez, 16–17

New York City, Frémonts in, 201, 237, 240, 241–243

New York *Evening Post*, 203–204, 223, 237

New York *Herald*, 165, 223, 234, 237

New York *Tribune*, 205, 223, 237; description of Frémont in, 149–150

Nicollet, Jean Nicholas, and Mississippi and Missouri rivers, 23, 26; expeditions of, 26–42; reports of, 43–44, 49; illness of, 44, 49; letter from, to Frémont, 47; death of, 109; *see also* mapmaking *and* astronomical calculations

"On Crossing the Rocky Mountains After Many Years," 247–248

Oregon, problems of, 112, 143

Oregon Trail, 50, 83, 113, 180

Osage, 76

Owens, Richard, and Carson, 118;

and 3rd expedition, 120, 126, 131; and fight with Indians, 134, 138; aids Frémont, 179

Paris, Frémonts in, 192–193, 216, 217, 241

Peak of the Hawk, 128–129

Phelps, William D., 149–150

Phillips, Wendell, 239

Pico, Don Rio, 129, 153

Pillow, Gen'l Gideon J., 219

Platte River, 54, 56, 63–67

Poinsett, Joel R., 15–16, 18, 21, 26, 43, 47

Polk, James Knox, 112, 113–114, 133, 166

Pope, Gen'l John, 231, 233

Prentiss, Gen'l Benjamin M., 219, 220

Preuss, Charles, and 1st expedition, 54, 63; and 2nd expedition, 72, 83, 85; and 3rd expedition, 120; and 4th expedition, 169, 174; and 5th expedition, 195

Price, Gen'l Sterling, 231, 233, 234

Provot, Etienne, 32, 34

railroads, proposed routes and construction of, 18, 51, 168–169, 185, 186, 194, 198, 199, 237, 238, 242–243

Renville, Joseph, 31, 42

Republican Party, formation of, 202; and slavery, *see* slavery; and Frémont, 203–211; and presidential candidates, 215, 237–239; composition of, 236

Rio Buenaventura, 101

Robertson, Dr. John, 12–13, 247

Sacramento (horse), 109, 115, 139

Sagundai, 115, 121, 139

St. Louis, description of, 27–28, 218; Frémonts in, 27–28, 31–32, 42, 51, 71, 104, 106–109, 115, 162, 218–232, 234; growth of, 106; Confederates and, 218, 220, 221; *see also* Missouri

San Bernardino, battle at, 154

San Diego, taking of, 154

San Francisco, *see* California *and* Yerba Buena
San Juan, taking of, 150
San Pascual, battle at, 154
Savannah, 146, 151
Scott, Winfield, 49, 231, 232
Seward, William H., 203
Seymour, Sir George, 150
Shoshones, 79–81
Sibley, Henry, 28–29, 31
Sierra Nevadas, 85–100, 105
Sigel, Col. Franz, 221, 233
Sioux, 29–31, 35, 40–41, 56
slavery, California and, 185; Frémont and, 185, 188, 201–202, 203, 211, 223–226; Democrats and, 187, 201–202, 207, 209; Republicans and, 202–203; *see also* Emancipation Proclamation
Sloat, John D., 146, 149, 151–152
Smith, Gerrit, 211
Smith, Jedidiah, 50
Snake Indians, 56, 83–84, 91–92
Snyder, Jacob R., 184
Solomon, Chief, 195, 196
Songs of Three Centuries, 247
South Pass, 50, 56, 59, 69, 80–81
Souvenirs of My Time, 244
Stanton, Edwin, 237
Staten Island, Frémonts in, 244, 245–246
Stockton, R. F., 152–160
Sublette, William, 50
Sumner, Charles, 224
Sutter, John Augustus, 97–98, 127, 142; and Frémont, 145; and Mexican War, 149; loses holdings, 180
Sutter's Fort, 97–100, 126, 127; U.S. flag over, 149; gold at, 180
Swanok, 115, 137

Tarrytown, Frémonts in, 240, 243
Taylor, Zachary, 134, 160, 183, 184
Texas, problems of, 111–112, 133, 143
Thomas, Lorenzo, 233
Tilden, Samuel J., 204
Todd, William L., 145–146
Torre, Joaquin de la, 146
Tyler, John, 49, 112

Union Army, *see* Civil War
U.S., and Columbia River, 69; and Mexico, *see* Mexico; and Oregon, 112; and California, 112, 115, 132; *see also* Congress and presidents
U.S. Topographical Corps, 18, 21
Upham, Charles W., 247

Van Buren, Martin, 21, 43
Victoria, Queen, 192

wagon trains, *see* emigrant trains
Walpole, Lt. Frederick, 150–151
Washburne, Elihu P., 233–234
Washington, D.C., description of, 26; Frémont in, 26–27, 32, 43–49, 67, 68, 109–115, 162, 186, 200, 201
Washington *Nat'l Intelligencer,* 200, 232
Webster, Daniel, 49
Wellesley, Marchioness of, 192
Wellington, Duke of, 192
West, settling of, 44, 49, 69, *see also* Frémont expeditions; errors in reports of, 113
Westport Landing, 168, 169, 194–196
Whig Party, 204–205, 210, 236
Whiting, Anne Beverly, 10; *see also* Frémont, mother of
Whitman, Marcus, 84, 87
Whittier, Elizabeth H., 208–209
Whittier, John Greenleaf, poems of, 105, 207–208, 209, 226; and Frémont campaign, 205, 207–208, 239–240; and Frémont's poem, 247
Wide Awake, 244
Wilkes, Charles, 85
Wilkins, William, 108
Will and the Way Stories, The, 244
Williams, "Old Bill," and 4th expedition, 170, 174, 177, 179, 194
Williams, W. S., 18, 19

Year of American Travel, A, 244
Yerba Buena, 149
Young, Brigham, 83

Zindel, Louis, 34, 38, 71